"You gave us a glimpse into your world of why you are now in a wheelchair for life. You chose to go ahead and tell the truth in order to perhaps help others get past those dreadful seasons of coping with all of those hidden emotions. You triumphed through all the obstacles, even though it was not easy to do so. This is your story of victory that I pray will motivate and encourage others.

Your story is proof that life is not over for the quadriplegic, it is a new season to adjust to and keeping moving forward. "

Sudie Landry
Writers' Guild of Acadiana
President

"3 Lifetimes In 1" the story of his life in despair, is courageously told and very focused with genuine emotion, capturing the attention of the reader throughout the entire book. A vivid memoir with great clarity and detail, tells an unforgettable survival story."

—Gwendolyn Reasoner Phd., National Award Winning Author of *"Where Did the Day Go?"*

"May all who read this be blessed."

3 Lifetimes In 1
A True Story About Change And Redemption

by

Mark Wayne Allen

**© 2016 by Mark Wayne Allen
All Rights Reserved**

Other Writings by Mark Wayne Allen

AWARDS AND PUBLICATIONS

Awards
First place poem Parish Fair - Life, The Miracle
Fourth Place (Writer's Conference)

Books
Novella - Star Siege

Publications
Dementia e-zine - This Land Is Your Land
Dementia e-zine - Johnny
Dementia e-zine - Discovery

Bayou Writers Group Anthology Vol. 2
Bayou Writers Group Anthology Vol. 1
15 Articles in "The Voice of Southwest Louisiana"

Foreword

This is a book that I have wanted to write for almost 10 years but never could figure out how. By how, I mean from what point of view, what to focus on, what manner do I write it, etc., plus I never felt the conviction to begin writing.

Most of all, I didn't want this book to offend anybody, hurt feelings, or bring up matters about each individual person that are better left unsaid. We all have aspects of our lives that we dread to reveal, right?

Another question was whether or not to include pictures.

I suppose the biggest reason that I have hesitated is because of my unending and vast emotional ties to the subject matter. I have been through some major traumas in my lifetime. I presume, more than most people even think is possible.

Most of us go through life at our station and do not go beyond the boundaries of what we know. My life has not been like that. It has been filled with one upheaval after the other. Alongside these tragic events, has been a collection of miracles.

Not long ago, I finally was led by God to fill this book up with memories based upon the theme that He wanted. The events in this book are real and have changed me over the years.

I have been molded into exactly what the good Lord wants me to be, or at least I'm assuming. I don't know what God's plan for me is, but I do know that I have been through some remarkable and miraculous changes over the course of time.

The contents of this book are His, but the words are mine. If you have any trouble with any part of this book blame me, not the architect.

The title was given to me in a dream and I woke up in the middle of the night with the notion of how to write this book.

If you are a person that has been in my life and you don't see your name in this book, there is a reason for that. First of all, this book has a focus and to that end I had to bring out some details and leave others behind. Superfluous details would have been a distraction. Secondly, to avoid possible offenses to people, all proper names have been changed to one or two letters which may not have any bearing on the person's actual identity.

I suffer from posttraumatic stress disorder (PTSD) due to the events that have occurred in my lifetime. Because of these stresses, a lot of the pages in this book ought to be tear-soaked. I wrote a lot of these words through a watery haze from the magnitude of the emotions involved. Yes, over the years I've learned to deal with these things in a healthy way, but any person, especially doctors, will tell you that reopening old injuries is problematic.

Actually *"magnitude"* is not the correct terminology. PTSD is more like scrambled nerves. The book gets into that in more detail so I won't go into it here.

Many years have passed since most of the events in this book, but that doesn't make the issues any less easy to deal with. In a way, that is a good thing I suppose. I always try to deal with events by adapting the best way I can and by developing a plan for going on with life.

I've been taught by God to enact a first response to any problem. I look at Him both for strength and answers and then go forward. That's really all we can do. Move forward…

To my beloved wife Kelley who dried my tears as I wrote

XII

3 Lifetimes In 1

My First Life

Mark Wayne Allen

1

The Beginning

Let me say something before I even start. Quite a number of people have asked me to write my life's story, but I've never been quite comfortable with the idea. The intensity of emotions that have been in my life have, at times, been all consuming and therefore tough to deal with on any level.

The intensity of which I speak may be hard for most to understand, but the depth of emotionalism have, at points, completely taken over my mind and life. Basically, I was an unwitting observer of things right in front of me. That kind of thing is tough for even me to understand, but I've had to deal with facts about myself and my life that is totally beyond anything that 95% of the population can even imagine.

There are some things I may find too difficult to put into words. That's okay. There are also things that I will take to the grave with me. That's okay too. I don't imagine all of anyone's life has ever been put into any book. What I'm saying to you, the reader, is that parts of my story will both be difficult to write and be might be disturbing to read. Be ye warned!

Mark Wayne Allen

> I hope you do continue because there's bound to be a lot of good times. You may even laugh at some things.
> Let's proceed, shall we?

*

My story actually starts long before my birth. My future parents had one son, which they adored, and wanted another child. They were young, active, and healthy people who were into almost everything outdoors. My Dad was a sportsman and my Mom, not being from a outdoor background, I think just did everything in order to be with him. She grew to love being an active woodsy sports-oriented person over the span of time and still talks about how much fun it was.

It was admirable of her, to be sure, and I'm certain that she loved being with him. They fished too, with poles from the bank and from boats. Hunting rabbits, squirrels, and especially ducks were their favorites.

They were your average, decent, young couple except for the fact that my Mom never learned to cook. She would fix him meals that a billie-goat would sneer at and he would eat it with a yummy smile in consideration of her feelings. He soon learned not to do that because if he said that he liked the meal, guess what, she would fix it again, again, and again. Anyway, I start with them because that's how life starts, right?

They had been trying to have me for almost four years and had almost given up when, BOOM! Mom finally got pregnant. They were ecstatic, as you might imagine, and told all of their friends and family. Who could blame them? They were both God-fearing souls who wanted to 'go forth and procreate.' To have another child in their lives would be a further blessing to them.

The pregnancy was normal in all respects and Mom and Dad both continued their hunting trips all the way into the her eight or ninth month. It kept her physically fit, which meant healthy and strong, which is always a good thing. It was especially so in her case as you will see later.

There is a thing that happened during her pregnancy that bears mentioning. I can't remember exactly at what stage she was, I think it was between six to seven months somewhere, but I think they were living in Merryville at the time, someone intruded into the house. Dad was suspicious about the event and contacted someone he knew. What he found out was amazing. A contract had been put out for my Mom's death. WOW! Anyway, he cleared the matter promptly and life went on.

I mention this for reasons that I'll explain much later, but regardless, it attests to an unsteady beginning for a young life.

Finally, we come to my birth. I was born in Merryville, Louisiana on February 8, 1966 at a small hospital that was across the street from where my maternal grandmother's home was. The house was, and is, a big, nice house, but that's really immaterial to my story, I just thought I'd mention it.

Sorry, my mind was gone for a while, but I'll continue my story now. It's funny how the mind works. I guess we need those little flashes of memories here and there to refresh our concentration.

Hours before I was born, my Mom went into one long, continuous contraction that lasted right up until I was born. If it had not been for the great shape that she was in, combined with a zero-weight-gain pregnancy, I'm not sure that neither of us would have survived the ordeal. The doctor agreed, apparently, because after it was over, he said, "no more". I'm quite sure that Mom was thinking, "Hell no! Never again! That's it! 'Finito! Final answer!!!"

I can't say I blame her. Can you? After experiencing an ordeal like that, I'm sure she was exhausted. Even to this very day, she says she'd have ten kids like my brother rather than one like me. You can easily see that my birth was unusual, in most respects, as my future lives were to be.

I once heard funny lady Carol Burnett conceptualize for us men what the act of giving birth was like. She said, "Pull your bottom lip OVER your head." Well, I'm quite sure that I don't want to do that. It would hurt! Pain hurts me. I choose to remain ignorant about the pains of birth.

*

Okay, so here I was in the world, alive and healthy. The day after my birth, my Mom went home to her Mom's, fifty yards from the hospital. She walked there. That was Mother. A strong woman and physically fit... Living beside the hospital obviously had its advantages.

When she got there, my Aunt Z (For the sake of anonymity, all proper names will be changed except mother, daddy, and brother) snagged me into her arms. She then insisted, relentlessly, that she be allowed to feed me my first bottle. My Mom fed one of her baby dolls. I can only assume it was to show Z how to do it, but she had probably been feeding dolls since she was two. After all, we quickly indoctrinate kids to gender-specific acts of life and behavior. We teach girls to bat their eyes at the boys and the boys to act like strong he-men, physically and emotionally. "Don't cry, suck it up," Dads tell us boys and, as a result, grown men hide their pain.

Ah, but back to my story.

> A CAVEAT: My brother was told throughout Mom's pregnancy that I was going to be a girl and that he was going to have a little sister. They built his hopes up big time! Well, when everyone found out that I was a boy, Michael was highly upset. He wanted a little sister as a sibling. So he, Mom, and Dad all had a little discussion, I assume, about their errors and how nice it would be to have a brother instead. So, he finally agreed that yeah, maybe having a little brother would be nice too.

Little did Michael realize what a little twerp I could be or what a best friend.

I was a good baby. I hardly ever cried. Dad worked hard at his job and often wound up coming home late at night. He could wake me up from a deep sleep, play with me a while, then put me back in my crib, and I would go right back to sleep. That was great for his long working hours and I wish it could be like that for other young Dads.

Not all babies are the same. *Thank God!* I was unusual in many respects, I suppose. That is, until my monster-side came out.

Every now and then we'd go to Granny's and spend the nights at her house. Each time we went, this great-mannered baby would turn into a combination of Frankenstein meets Godzilla: loud, cranky, and annoying. Crying every minute of the day and night, I commanded the attention of whoever could hear the "good baby" screaming at the top of my lungs. It put new meaning to the words "ear shattering".

Well, apparently I was miserable, really miserable, and I was determined to make everyone else as weary from what I was upset about. Anyone who's been around a cantankerous baby knows exactly what I mean. I was teary-eyed and blaring.

Time and time again, I would be the perfect baby at home, but go to Granny's house, and here comes *Frankenzilla*! It was a terrible state of affairs...

UNTIL

One night when we came home from misery-incognito and I was laid to sleep, Mom and Dad (I don't know who was first) came in the crib room and noticed something. I just so happened to be laying down coo'ing and goo'ing and rubbing the bed like it was a long-lost-friend that I loved.

3 Lifetimes In 1

From that moment on, whenever we went to Granny's, Dad would disassemble then re-assemble that cotton-pickin' crib.

A NOTE TO THE UNWARY: Have you ever put together a baby bed??? Let me tell you something, Friends. I have assembled radios, tents, lawnmowers, and everything else you can think of. ***There ain't NOTHING as COMPLICATED as a #!^&%)(*& baby bed!!!***

When I was a teenager, my Dad, who was an engineer of sorts, and two other men, who were equally qualified, tried to put one of these crazy, mishmash things together for six-hours one day and FAILED! The next day, I spent THE ENTIRE DAY trying to put this thing together.

I started working on "<u>the thing</u>" at 9 A.M., stopped long enough to get lunch, and worked some more right up until 6 P.M. The instructions on those things read like they were originally written in Japanese, translated into Chinese, then into German, then back to Japanese, and finally transcribed by a Brazilian into English. Every teeny-tiny little part has an essential purpose.

Pardon me, but it's crazy. Pay no attention to the ravings of a madman. Those things just make me so frustrated and I'm not easily flustered.

Anyway, after they saw me caressing my bed, Dad said, "That's it! The baby bed goes with us every time from now on!" So that was the deal. Every time we went to stay with Granny, that baby bed went with us. It may have been a nightmare, but it was not as much of one as me without it.

Grandpa, even back then, had a video camera, I think they called it 8mm film, with which he filmed the entire family: Granny, Aunt Z, his sons (my three uncle's), as well as Mom, Dad, and all my other family, and even distant relatives including friends. Granny had six kids altogether: three boys and three girls. I didn't know until much later, but one girl and two of the boys were from a previous marriage in which the guy died. I don't know why he died, I just know he died. She married my Grandpa a few years afterward. He was a merchant Marine and, as you can expect, had the mouth of a sailor. He was a nice guy really, but ill mannered, brash, and larger-than-life. Being the captain of a ship, however, I guess he had to be.

My brother, Michael, had a Batman fetish. He would go around everywhere attacking everybody and trying to do good deeds with his cape and mask, but Aunt Z was always his archnemesis. With her being bigger than him, she would always manage to throw him off or something. Now Uncle Y was also the comedian and, apparently, the one that always knew best. (You know the type, a prankster and fun to watch on film).

I said all this to tell you that I was in some of these films as an infant but I always felt kind of slighted although I know that's not true. I've always been rather envious of the good times that were captured in their young life. I know that it's merely a matter of timing and I was too young at the time, but things like that are a treasure. I mean my aunts and uncles, virtually all of them, can always go back and look at those films and say "hey, that was me".

Our family took pictures. And when I say "pictures", I mean, A LOT of pictures!!! I suppose that we all feel like we've missed out on something that others have had, that's just one of mine.

Mark Wayne Allen

2

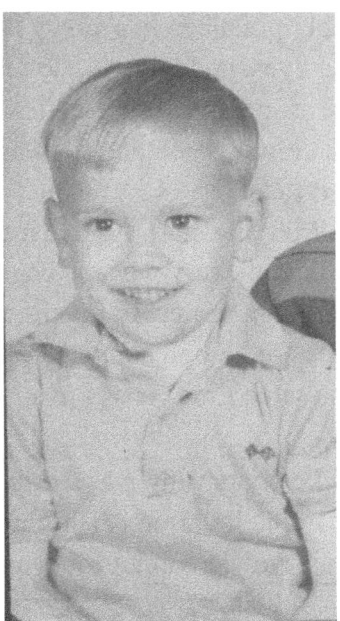

Young Life

    After the baby stage, came my beginning years of course. I crawled on the floor an unusually long time. I did not make the fumbling faltering steps that most kids do when they are learning to walk, you know, *baby's first steps*. The delay between crawling and walking was so long that everyone started to worry, but when I finally started walking, there were no fumbling steps but full strides.

    People have always been confused by that, but it makes sense to me. Knowing the way I am, I don't like to show anything off until I have it perfected. It's the same way that I did magic tricks. I practiced extensively and perfected a trick before I ever showed it to anybody. That's just me.

I probably practiced in secrecy, away from everybody and their prying eyes, and honed it down to a fine art before walking in front of people. They say I would still drop down to the floor and crawl someplace if I was in a hurry.

I learned to talk the same way. I started talking full sentences right from the start. As a matter fact, I took so long in starting to talk that everyone was beginning to wonder if there was something wrong. By the time I did talk, I had a hold on the basics of a good conversation. That's both unique and weird at the same time. That's me.

That's like yours truly was a dog for a while. You read that right and I wrote it correctly. I didn't pretend I was a dog, I became a dog. I crawled on all fours and ate out of a bowl on the floor.

It became so bad that Mom became worried. She took me to the doctor. This dog tagged along without a leash. Doc said that it was *a sign of intelligence...* he he he (I agree)... and not to worry about it.

But, as fate would have it, the dog started chasing cars. Really! I'm serious! Dad spanked this puppy over that and that was the end of the dog, but it only came after my invisible friend Robert (pronounce rObert, with a long O).

Robert became so ingrained into my life that we had to set a place for him at the dinner table. One day Daddy came into the kitchen and sat down. Well, this young kid

3 Lifetimes In 1

> started screaming, "Get up! Get up!" He was sitting on Robert.
>
> Now, I think everyone will agree, I was an Angel kid. Yeah, that's right, my horns held up my halo. Robert did all the bad stuff, it was all his fault. Everything was his fault. He even peed on the toilet seat. In fact, he was bad about doing that.
>
> I don't remember when he disappeared, but eventually he did.

Back before my memory kicks in comes another pretty gross tale that my Mom tells about how one day my brother and I got pretty quiet. She said she didn't think much about it. She knew we were all right because we were giggling. But, as most of us know, when kids get quiet, you better go check on them.

I have no idea how long we were in the kitchen alone, but it was long enough. By the time she walked in, the kitchen was destroyed. There she saw her lovable two kids who had gotten into the old grease and had spilled it out on the floor. We would run and slide in the grease and just thought it was the funniest thing in the world. The walls, as high as our hand could reach, were all caked in grease. And so were the chairs and the cabinets and the drawers and the knobs and whatever else that you can think of.

Apparently, she took mercy on us. After all, neither of us knew any better. We were too young. Nevertheless she was aghast. I can relate to that. *What a mess*!!!

Well, I think she spent the entire rest of the day cleaning us and our greasy diapers up, along with the entire rest of the kitchen. Young kids... Ah, to be young again.

I barely remember it, but I had a habit of going under the house although Mom didn't want me to. Time and time again, I would go under the house to play. I was just a young kid and didn't realize the dangers of going under house and it, apparently, terrified Mom! Now as luck would have it, I hated water in my face. I don't know what it was, but water in my face used to terrify me. It felt like a water district going into my nose and no matter what I did and I wouldn't be able to breathe. I would just be sitting there drowning in my fear.

It wasn't true, of course, but it was still a scary thing to a young kid. Well, my Mom knew this and sort of turned the tables on me.

She had told me and told me, but it did no good, as it does oftentimes with children. So one day she came outside while I was underneath and she grabbed a water hose, turned it on, and sprayed right in my face. Well, as young kid, I started screaming. She just insisted that I come out from under there. I started bawling and wailing as I crawled out swiftly and, most assuredly, never went back in or, rather, back under. It was a tough lesson, but worth it.

Now this same woman was also the one who nurtured me in the pool that we had. I don't know how big it was, but it seemed big to a very young kid like me. Well, Michael and me were in that pool for what seemed like a long time.

3 Lifetimes In 1

Michael was having a lot of fun and was trying to incorporate me in on that, which I appreciated.

With my feet not even touching the bottom and a horrible fear of water in my face, the time passed rapidly for me I suppose.

I got cold and very tired of working my way around the edge of the pool trying to hang with my big brother. The metal band at the top was beginning to hurt my cold hands. My dear, sweet, Mom bent down, ever so gently, and held out her hands saying, "Baby, why don't you and I go in?"

I really felt comforted that evening. I know she was enjoying the outdoors, but here she was at my side offering companionship and comforting love while her counterpart helped my brother. I gladly went into her helping hands and arms. Soaked and miserable I went in with her after she dried me off. I had my fun, gone far beyond, and was thankful it was over. Many times after that I looked back at the small above ground pool decaying in our yard and remembered that evening.

Those are the things that make and show love. This was one of those times that you remember for a lifetime. It was so warm and comforting and it did my heart good to feel those warm arms, to have a Mom's love surround me.

When we were living in Merryville still, one of my first memories is that my Mom and granny sitting in the living room of the house, which incidentally was right across the street from my Uncle's place, and I was rubbing my forehead against the metal screen of an open window and felt like I was making an impression of the cross–hatches of the screen.

I don't know why I did this, but I was sure having fun doing it. Granny seemed so pleased, evidenced by her smiles, so that prompted me to carry on. I don't know how long this went on, but it was at least until Granny left. Everyone liked my Granny. She was a nice, humble, woman without any axes to grind about anybody. If she ever talked bad about anyone, I never knew it.

That kind of woman, or person, should be celebrated.

Living where we did gave me the opportunity to make friends with a cousin. He was a little bit younger than me, but that didn't stop us from developing a great friendship. We would play all the time with each other: cars, trucks, games, and everything in between. It is a shame that we got distanced when our family moved away. Oh, it did not happen all at once, but it did happen. Although we're almost strangers now, I still like him very much and, family being what it is, would help him anytime he asked me to.

He is an easy-going chap with a college education now. I still call him a friend. Good friends are often hard to find in this world. That's like we had some good friends from almost 30 years ago recently come. They came from a long distance and were welcomed with open arms.

Once I make a friend, something extraordinary has to happen for me to ever change my mind in the least bit. It's a lesson all of us should learn: *the value of good people*. I'm not referring to value that you can monetize or assess in power.

3 Lifetimes In 1

The affairs of the heart are not like that. The emotions of joy and love keep our spirits uplifted and add to the quality of our lives.

> *NOTE TO READER: I know it seems like I am veering off of the beaten path a lot, but the first few years of anyone's life sets the stage for future years. My future life is extremely turbulent and the qualities that make me the person I am today, or comprise my value system, as a psychologist would say, are very important.*

When we moved away to Abbeville (or was it Belle Chase), Louisiana, (near New Orleans anyway) we lived in an apartment complex and there was this boy that lived there. We'll call him C. He was one of those friends that you like and dislike. There was an interesting thing about the kid, he only had one full arm. The other one had a birth defect. Just below the elbow, it stopped. He had tiny nubs for fingers.

Actually, you couldn't really consider them fingers (although he did), they were more like tiny blobs to me. He said he could use them, but I don't necessarily believe that and I never did. In fact, now that I'm older, I can't see where they would be of any use to anybody.

Anyway, we got along fairly well most of the time, but every once in a while, we would get into a heated discussion or an outright disagreement and fight like cats and dogs. It makes me a little bit ashamed to say, even today, that when we would fight, he would kick my tail every time. How he could use that one arm so very efficiently is beyond me.

I guess that just goes to show you what people with disabilities can do when they put their mind to it. Today, I know that for sure, now. Some people around me don't even see how I keep up with my daily life. Well, it's like this, you always make the best of what you have and then let the chips fall where they may. If you come up short, you can always say,' *"Well, I tried my best."*

When we moved out of that apartment complex, I was both sad and happy that I would be away from that kid. With medical technology the way it is, I'm sure he has a prosthetic arm by now. Bravo, for him!

I started and finished preschool when we lived near New Orleans. Like every kid I guess, I was so very nervous the first day. Mother consoled me and told me that I was going to be all right. I remember that every morning we would pass by a building, I don't know which one, but it had a small Air Force jet mounted on a podium of sorts. Inside the cockpit, there was a flight suit sitting in the chair.

As a young boy who didn't know better, I let my imagination run away with me and I was convinced that there was a man inside the flight suit. I always thought how cool it was for a person to actually be sitting in the cockpit. Of course, there was nobody in the flight suit, but I did not realize that. How preposterous something like that would be! I didn't realize that at the time of course, but every morning I would study that cockpit carefully watching for signs of movement and never saw any. Too bad!

3 Lifetimes In 1

Anyway, pre-K was a lot of fun because of lots of arts and crafts. My teacher, I forget her name, was one of those boisterous, bouncy, happy-go-lucky types that were really good with kids and I quickly became one of her favorites I think. Maybe it was just my charisma, but more than likely my imagination…

> At the risk of self-incrimination and with a sense of common decency, I will tell you that I am a murderer. Yes, that's right, I said a murderer! I am a merciless torturer also. I have tortured and mangled scores of cockroaches and doodlebug's. With the cockroaches, I would pull off their legs and their wings, set them aside, and eat the bodies. Yes, I said eat them. I did not like the wings or the legs. The roly-poly's (or doodlebugs), I played with and thereafter ate. I even brought a handful of them to my Mom and asked her to cook them because they were so good raw.
>
> Yes, I know. It sounds gross and she said no, of course. To a little kid who didn't know any better though, it made sense. As justification, these bugs are a good source of protein. Hey, I have to make sense of my unusualness somehow!
>
> Also, have you ever microwaved a cockroach? It won't die! It just crawls around and looks at you. Weird!

Shortly after completing preschool, we moved to North Carolina. It was an awfully long way from Louisiana and when we got there, the road we were on ended at an oceanfront pier. I suppose it was a sightseeing adventure to Mom and Dad, but I reacted quite differently.

When I saw the ocean, I started bawling my eyes out and screaming, " I knew it!!! I knew it!!! We've come to the end of the world!!!" It was very dramatic for me at the time. Still today, I laugh at it and so does everyone else, mainly because it is so ridiculous. I suppose a little bit of it is because you are getting to see the world from a much smaller viewpoint.

The world is always much bigger to a child. Everything is larger than life from the smaller perspective. It is not necessarily immaturity that makes a child's point of view be so distorted, but children are very small in comparison to the rest of the world.

There was a house that we moved into that I remember pretty well. It was the beginning of the school year and being in kindergarten, I got home early. Mom was sewing bits of carpet together at the time, for what reason I don't know. Well, I wanted to help. So she taught me how to hand stitch, as she was doing, and we sewed together. I was pretty good with my hands and soon picked up the technique.

Well, I was enjoying it, but then I heard the bus. "Michael's home," I shouted, and, in kid fashion, instead of just dropping the project, used up all of my thread very quickly. This entailed making the biggest sewing loops that you ever saw (two-inch loops or more), but once I started a job, I was going to finish. Unfortunately, the good job that I was doing was marred by a horrible stitching at the end.

Now, understand, Mother probably didn't need or want the piece that I was doing. She probably knew what was going to happen, but still, I remember it, and feel like I let her down. That episode was akin to my going to a friend's birthday party, being masked, and pinning the tail on a donkey. There was a pinhole in the mask that I could see through. I won, naturally, but have never forgotten the hollowness in my gut that I felt afterward.

> Those kinds of things stick with you years after the events. They help shape us and build our character. Yes, kids will be kids, and it depends on the values instilled by one's parents. For me, those things made me unhappy with my conduct.

NOTATION: I didn't let anybody down cleaning fish however. I was actually too little to help clean so my job became getting the eyeballs out with a spoon. I wasn't going to watch everybody work and not do my best to help. I always grabbed my tool and gouged at those wobbly little things. I never seemed to get all of them because they simply told me that that was enough and grabbed the last fish.

I was a diligent servant though and was proud of it. **Hey, at least I was a team player!**

We had to move from our pretty little house when summer arrived because of in-season rates versus off-season.

It was a beautiful house surrounded by white sands. Ah, but we moved into a nice trailer house.

When I entered first grade things began to heat up, especially on the bus ride home. I don't remember if it was M or A that I had trouble with, but they were two brothers, sort of like Michael and I. They were approximately the same ages.

Now, let me explain something before I continue. In North Carolina, every kid of every age rode the same school bus from seniors to kindergarten and if a fight broke out, the bus driver was stopped the vehicle and put the kids off to finish fighting. The loser had to walk home.

> Barbaric as it was, that was the deal the entire time we lived there. I'm sure that has changed, now that we live in a more civilized society. Ha! That's a hoot! Human nature is a really vile thing for a lot of people. Kids are excused because as my brother has said they get smarter up until they are 13 and then lose their brains until they are 20.

Anyway, this kid, I think it was A, every time he got off the bus in the afternoon, he would come up behind me, and shove me in the back. To anyone, that would get annoying and I told the bus driver just like I should, multiple times in fact, but it did no good. So finally, about halfway through the school year, he shoved me in the back one time too many and I came up out of my seat.

<u>My brother and me, we had a rule</u>. If bigger kids picked on me, then he would take care of it and, if smaller

kids picked on him, I would take care of it. When I came up out of my seat, my brother figured "Here we go." A was a fifth grader and much bigger than me. This little first grader commenced to beating on him with a fury.

By the time it was all over, that fifth grader had been beaten to a pulp by me and me alone. It may have not been important to anybody else but me, but at least I showed him that there are people who do fight back and won't be subjugated by overwhelming power. I often wonder if that minor incident helped change in his life for the good. That's a question that I'll never know the answer to, like so many other questions from my youth.

By the way, me, nor Michael ever walked home.

Later on, they would end up dividing the grades per bus. It was really for the best. Having everybody on one bus is really a bad idea. Ah, but then came another problem. I was a very dynamic kid who sexually matured the moment I was born. Although I didn't know all the facts, I was promiscuous. At least, to the extent of an innocent young boy who really didn't know anything except kissing...

Sitting in the backseat of the bus was like a status symbol to us kids. Only the most popular kids got to sit in the back of the bus. Well, when they divided up the bus by age groups, I was one of the older kids and would sit in the back of the bus along with all the girls. There, I turned into an underage Casanova and would play kissing games with the girls. The girls loved it! I, of course, did too. We would be kissing each other from the time the bus left the school to the time that I got off.

Now, after a while, my brother Michael, got jealous (*at least that's my story*). Actually, I don't know where his mind was but he told Mom and Dad that I was chasing them down and then forcefully kissing them. Perhaps I was. I'm not really sure, but it was all a game to me AND the girls, were loving it! Anyway, Dad talked to me and that pretty much ended the kissing games. I suppose it was for the best.

In the first grade, I was in an experimental classroom. There were three first grade classes that were open at all times and we were free to come and go at will. We got our assignments in one room and then went to different areas to work. As long as we reached certain target goals in each subject by a certain time, we could do whatever we wanted with the rest of the time.

By the end of the first grade, I was in a fifth grade reader and was caught up in every other subject. I loved it! I was (and still am) an independent, self-motivated person anyway. You let me go at anything on my terms and I'll excel every time.

Sadly, they canceled the program and I spent the second grade feeling confined. I was fidgety as well.

When we moved to the second trailer, life was much better. We had a tremendous size yard! I'm talking like 5 acres maybe. On the side of the house, in the midst of some pine trees, we began digging some foxholes.

> Now we liked to play with army men and, for one Christmas, got Army task forces. It was a tremendous boost to our militia. At that time, every spare nickel that we got when into buying army men, trucks, and equipment. I'm talking about the little plastic replicas that they used to sell everywhere. The sets that we got more than double the size of our army.

Anyway, in addition to playing with these army men, we dug huge foxholes and had dirt clod wars. The dirt around North Carolina was very moist and you could make dirt clods very easy. Sometimes we would have dirt clod wars. It was a lot of fun. The clods broke apart easy when they hit so the only real hazard was dirt in the eyes. Not fun...

Michael was more industrious that I was. He would dig his foxhole *very deep*. Sometimes he would help me dig mine out, but then he would return to deepening his, down to the water table. I'm talking six-feet down! He'd have to create dirt steps to get it in and out.

It is a wonder that he didn't end up trapped down there it was so deep, but he had to stop when his foxhole began became more like a well. Later on, we moved locations in the yard and we created a tunnel system with one foxhole on each end with a trench in between. In the middle of the two foxholes, we dug a reservoir and filled it with dirt clods and pinecones.

We would throw them at each other in the guise of playing war. The brown pinecones were okay, but the green ones were hard, sticky, and they hurt like crazy, but if we were desperate, we would use them.

Later on, we dug a tremendous size foxhole that we both fit in easily with lots of room to spare. It had a bridge in the middle too. Now, we had a rule that nobody walked across the bridge when somebody was underneath. As the best laid plans often go, one day somebody came over and Michael wanted to show off the bridge and its strength. I was underneath doing something and Michael bounced up and down on top of the bridge.

I fully understand that he was trying to show off for our guests. Rules are rules though. Isn't fate is a fickle thing? As you can guess, the 6-inch thick dirt bridge gave way and I was buried under a mountain of dirt unable to move.

Michael started looking around, didn't see me, and then started hearing the faint noise of my screaming (so I guess I was getting a little air at least). Looking around, he began to see my feet kicking. Well, he dug me out, and then had to run as I was screaming at him at the top of my lungs, mad as a firecracker.

In all honesty, I really don't blame him, although I like to pick at him about the incidence. It was an honest mistake and he dug me out as quickly as he could.

It horrified Dad when he came out back one day and saw that nearly the entire back yard had been dug up. It took lots of hours to dig all of that up. Much later, it was discussed that if we had ever been asked to do that much work, it would have never gotten done.

Speaking of W-O-R-K reminds me of

THE YARD

It was one of the major incidents that I had when I was a kid. Now understand, Michael and I saved up soft drink bottles, which in those days had a five cent deposit on them, for weeks at a time and then loaded them up in wagons. We would then walk them up to the local convenience store and cash them in. We used the money to buy drinks and snacks to be consumed during the walk home. Industrious of us, don't you think?

We were into fishing also. There were two ponds a little ways behind where we lived. Almost daily we would dig up worms and go fishing. In other words, we were into anything and everything, but didn't really care for work.

Now, in 1972 my Dad offered us $50 apiece to clean up our yard and gave us a whole month to do it in. That by itself was very generous, but us boys chose to ignore the yard in favor of fun activities. Well, four weeks rolled by and we had done nothing on the yard, so Dad offered us $25 apiece and gave us two more weeks.

Well, as you might expect, we were into crawfishing and generally fun stuff like games too much as we ignored the warnings for another two weeks. Well, at the end of this timetable, he said now we were doing it for free and gave us another week. Yet another week went by and we did nothing. He came home one day and asked us if the job had been completed. Of course we had to say no. He took out his belt and you can imagine what happened next.

Sobbing, we went out to the yard as per his instructions and started cleaning up. Well, 10 minutes later, we came back in and said it was done. He went outside with us and inspected our work. As you can imagine, there were about 100 things that we didn't do and what we had done wasn't done correctly. Guess what, he told us what we did wrong and whipped us again.

So, we had another chance to get it right. Well, 10 minutes later we came back in and said it was done. He inspected again, told us what we did wrong, and whipped us once more.

I don't know and nobody in the family knows just how many times that this went on, but by the end of it, we were all crying, sobbing, and defeated. But, to Dad's credit, once he laid down the gauntlet, he had to follow through no matter what.

It ended up being that we finished the job the next day. I didn't like it, but it was so dark that we could barely see anyway. I hated this demise, but I can tell you now that my Dad, by following through, did the right thing. He and Mom, however much they cried about doing what was right that night, always said that thereafter they were very careful about ultimatums and, I must say, learned a lot about them too.

There are so many of these childhood memories such as going down almost a mile away to an old dilapidated bridge to do some crawfishing, having Christmas's with lots of gifts and then sitting back, listening to Elvis Christmas music with the family, having disc gun wars inside the house, playing Monopoly at the table until the wee hours of the morning, how the pet alligator bit everyone but died when it bit Mom (*something we still tease her about*), all of those times when Michael and I would play Star Trek, fishing at creeks, badminton, planting and keeping gardens, fish tanks, pets, and all else in my early youth.

IMPORTANT:
There is one more thing that I would like to mention. I will be forever grateful to my Dad for reading books on child-rearing. From his readings, came the notion that most kids grow-up somewhat introverted. The books pointed to the premise that this was not a good thing. He decided that we would be better able to adapt to the world if we got beyond that.

So one night, he came in from work and we started doing pantomimes to songs that we were already familiar with. He wasn't particular about the songs that we used, mind you, he just wanted us to be able to get up and "perform" at least in front of each other.

At first, not surprisingly, we all declined the invitation, especially Michael and I. Well, he put on an Elvis tune and started performing for us. Soon, Mom got up there too and then, after a lot of coaxing and performing for several nights, Michael and I joined in with songs that we liked.

Soon, that got to be a nightly event, especially on weekends. When friends and neighbors would come over, we would try to get them to join in with us. At first, everybody was reluctant. Hey, forget reluctant, they were downright terrified. By that time though, we didn't really understand their fear. I mean, it had become second nature to us. We had lost our performance anxiety, at least in front of family and friends.

That has served me well over the years. I believe that, given my nature of isolationism that it would have been nearly impossible for me to confront the issues that would be forced on me in later years if not for those silly pantomimes.

There is a second reason that I'm thankful for these experiences. I was able to see, even in something as a two to four minute song, people interpret lyrics and the world, differently. People are all different and from varying backgrounds, thus their viewpoints are as unique as fingerprints.

3

Later Years As A Kid

The move from North Carolina to Texas changed everything for us. It even took us three days just to get there. It was rough on the body, as you can expect, but I think it was rough on the mind too. When you're cooped inside a tin can for days, it gets on your nerves and you become snappy. *It's not a pretty sight.*

It took a lot of courage on my Dad's part to even move us the great distance from Louisiana to North Carolina. I

think it took even more courage to move us all way to Texas. In neither move did we know what to expect and although we were closer to home in Texas, or what we consider our home base in Merryville, Louisiana, it was still halfway across the country and to a territory that we didn't have any inkling about except what the people that hired Dad had told us, or rather, him.
Courage, indeed!

After we got to Glen Rose, we found it to be the land of the dinosaurs. There were dinosaur tracks everywhere, especially in the riverbeds. It was sort of a touristy town, small, but with delightful people that we would soon grow to love.

We found a trailer in Rainbow, Texas just a short ways from Glen Rose, with the unique quality of having a split level where mine and Michael's bedrooms were. The top room was full-size while the bottom had a quarter-height. It was as wide and long as the top, but not very tall.

At first, I took the upstairs bedroom because we were arguing about it and so he finally let me have it. Ah, but brothers being brothers, he had a plan, which worked. He wound up doing some neat things with this downstairs hovel such as wallpapering the whole area with his decorative artwork, turning one of the two bed units into a display for his collectibles and books, and hanging up all kinds of neat little items. It was a regular man (*ahem*), boy, cave.

3 Lifetimes In 1

Now, brothers being envious of each other by nature, I thought this was neat-o and wanted to switch rooms and so he got what he wanted anyway. Soon, after switching, I realized what he did, but you might say I was committed because I had asked to switch rooms. I didn't mind though. The room was still neat and I did some interesting things with it myself too.

Outdoors, the first thing we did is tried to dig foxholes, the same as we did in North Carolina, but CLANG!!! After digging, or trying to, in several locations, we soon arrived at the conclusion that our efforts were in vain. The whole area was made of rock shale. If we were going to dig foxholes around here, we would need pickaxes and a lot of muscles.

So, we gave up on the idea of foxholes and started doing other things. We were each other's best friends by far. We had other friends too, but given the amount of time that we would spend together and how well we got along, we knew each other really well and liked one another. I often think about those young years doing things with Michael, and, let me tell you, they were some of the best times of my life.

It's kind of funny if you think about it. Your brother, or your sibling, is your best friend? Who would have ever thought that was possible? I don't know. It just seemed natural to us. Mom and Dad always made us get along well with each other, but that did not make us friends. Working together didn't make us friends either, much less best friends.

Shared respect, commitment, memories, love, and a deep rooted history of working toward our mutual betterment is what has made us this way and, I suppose, all best friends.

Still, today, even though we have separate lives and families, we each know that we can count on one other if for some reason we can't count on anybody else.

That's an amazing thing! We never have to talk in depth anymore, but we know that our bond exists and always will. Yes, we have had our differences in the past, both younger and older, but the bond between us will never go away. I wish all siblings could get along the way we did growing up. I wish everyone could feel this and have that kind of relationship.

Anyway, in lieu of foxholes, we started doing other stuff together. One of our favorite things to do was play football and wrestle as we had done so many times in North Carolina. We had been watching a lot of Mid-Atlantic wrestling back then. My favorite was Paul Jones and his was Wahoo McDaniel, the Indian chief. One time, we actually got to see McDaniel wrestle in person against The Minnesota Wrecking Crew.

We were so close to the ring that we had sweat droplets flying out of ring and hitting us. I was an excitable seven-year-old I guess and when Wahoo was attacking one of the guys, I would stand, jump up and down, and yell, "Kill him! Kill him!" Mom pulled on my arm, and said, "Mark, calm down, calm down." I was so unfocused that I started yelling, "Mark, calm down! Mark, calm down!"

3 Lifetimes In 1

It's funny if you think about. Wrestling was our main thing to do in North Carolina. I'm sure Michael spent a lot of the time trying not to hurt me. (After all, there is 4 and 1/2 years between us) My favorite hold was a headlock, only the way I did it was more like a stranglehold around the neck, and I would put every bit of strength that I had into it. Michael kept telling me that it was around the head, not the neck, but I guess I knew that he was bigger than I was and I was trying to incapacitate him any way that I could. It is a wonder that I didn't kill him by breaking his neck, but I guess God looks after little children.

Anyway, as we got older, the wrestling kind of faded, especially since it was not televised in our area, and we started playing football a lot. Sometimes it was tackle, other times it was tag. We could throw the ball just so far and it would be marked at the spot that it hit the dirt, but mostly it was a running game.

Now, we had a rule, I guess Michael had a rule that we always marked forward progress at the knees and where they came down. I think my brother bent the rule, or more like mangled it, when it suited his benefit. I mean this is the guy who also told me that the hot Sun heated sand, which I guess it does, and that cooked a sand crab. *Can you believe I actually ate one of those things on his say-so?*

I should say, 'tried to eat' because it was totally disgusting and I spit it out promptly.

Now that I backtracked a few years and thoroughly confused you, I'll continue with my story of Texas.

Instead of foxholes, wrestling, army men, fishing, and all sorts of fun and games, Michael and I got involved with other stuff. He began selling Grit magazine while I got into stereos and electronics.

There is an interesting story surrounding that. Dad had a friend, we'll him G, and we had went to his house to barbecue a few times. Well, we went there for Easter one year because the trailer we were living in did not have a big yard. It was fairly small and didn't have many places to hide eggs.

G lived down on the river and had about a half-acre yard so we went down there and barbecued, hid eggs, and generally had fun. Mom, Dad and, I guess, G, hid the eggs the first time, after that, Michael and I took turns hiding them from each other. It was loads of fun that day! Anyway, G barbecued for us what he called sugar steaks which sounds a little odd, but trust me, they are delicious!

After it turned dark and we all went inside, I started admiring the stereo system that G had. It was four units that were that were stacked on separate shelves in a decorative cabinet with four great big speakers attached to them. It may have been the lights that drew my attention. I don't know. I was always the one to park myself by or in front of Mom and Dad's stereo or in front of the speakers.

Other people, in a comparison to me, *liked music*. I **LOVED MUSIC** and still do. Well, as the evening went on, all of us talked a little bit and I got to where I really liked G. Later on, Michael went to sleep and I walked off to watch the stereos. One was not lit up and there was one over to the side on the floor.

Now, excuse me, but all kids lack tact. When G came over to where I was, I asked him what the one on the floor was. He told me that he had been trying to fix it because the one that was not lit up would not operate the speakers he wanted it to. Well, kids being kids, I asked him point-blank, if he got the one he wanted fixed, then could I have the other one.

Yes, it was very bold! I knew it was ill mannered and I was raised better than that, but I just couldn't help myself. G took it well though. First, he thought a moment, then said that if he could fix the other unit, then he would give that one to me. I was positively giddy inside at the mere thought of having that stereo. The one that I currently had, if you could call it that, was my Aunt E's old record player. It was nice and all. It was the kind that was like a suitcase with a handle that you opened up that the speakers were on the sides.

Well, a couple of days went by and G had not called or anything. That weekend, he was invited to dinner and when he knocked at the door, I rushed to it, and swung it open just like a kid waiting for Christmas. G stood at the doorway, hands beside his chest, and the amplifier in between. That night, if he would've gave me a choice between $8000 and the stereo that he brought, hands down I would've chosen the stereo.

Not only did he bring the amplifier, he brought an eight-track player, turntable, and a set of speakers. To me, they could have been liquid gold and not meant any more to me. I was touched beyond belief and as I relay this, I cannot help but tear up. Part of it is pride I suppose that someone outside of the family thought enough of my good sense of decency and well manners to give something like that to me. The other part is I guess that was the first mutual friendship that I established that was of an adult nature. *I'm probably rambling and I apologize, but my self-worth from that moment shot up about 1000%.*

> The first record that I ever played on that system was by the Steve Miller band, *Fly Like An Eagle*, which I bought myself. The second record that I ever bought was by the Captain and Teneille, *Muskrat Love*. I definitely remember those two because I bought them both on my own with my "not so hard earned" money and played them to death. I imagine everybody in the house remembers them too.

I still have that amplifier today and use it and often think about G. The eight-track player was the first to go down, then the record player, and finally the speakers, but that amplifier is still kicking. G, wherever you are, I salute you for taking an interest in that young kid long ago. *Thank you!*

We went to his house not long after that and I looked for the unit that he had "fixed" only to discover his generosity. G had given me the equipment of his own accord.

He had not repaired the other thing at all, but decided to bring joy to a young boy.

That friendship would continue throughout my life.

We did a lot of fishing in Glen Rose also. *Squaw Creek* was a favorite spot of ours, but after the nuclear power plant drew in most of the surrounding water from the river's and creeks, it ruined the fishing. The areas that were beautiful with life became snake-infested dens of diseased still water.

I have seen that happen over and over again. People **DO NOT** realize what these plants, whether it be a paper mill or whatever, do to the environment. If I had not personally witnessed the changes in the areas that we lived in, I would not have believed it.

Well, I guess I will get off of my soapbox. Besides, nobody would believe it anyway. Simply put, it is not the people that mattered. Why is it that the people with power often do not use it for the betterment of mankind? Heck, forget mankind, help the area that that you live in.

There was a girl that lived in a trailer beside us that I played with that we'll call A. She and I would play quite a bit and mostly we would play like we were gymnasts. She was a big fan of Nadia Komanietzsche and would try to imitate her gymnastic moves almost exactly. I never saw much sense in playing that way, but she liked it, so okay, I played with her the way she wanted.

Soon, she moved away and with Michael getting pretty much into his own affairs and girls. I went on with school and my life. That is, until I met M from the other fourth-grade class.

> Before I go into that, I probably should tell you about fourth-grade. North Carolina schools, on the whole, were ranked last in the nation at the time. Texas, their school system was ranked number one. As you might imagine, it was a very rough transition. Texas was writing cursive and they had known their multiplication tables ever since beginning third grade and I didn't know anything about either one. I was behind in a lot of subjects.
>
> The dedication and diligence of my teacher was, on the whole, very instrumental in helping me learn this stuff that was totally foreign to me. I had to spend long hours of very hard work just to try and catch up. I will never forget Mrs. K's tutelage and help.

Anyway, this girl, M, was my first crush. I remember her face and her long black hair just like it was yesterday. She lived in a house just down the road. We knew each other from school because we were in the same grade, different classes.

Anyway, she and her friend L would ride horses along the river just behind us. I would go with them a lot of times. We had a lot of fun and I fell in love. Like every young kid, I thought it was the real thing, but it soon died off.

I guess I was in love with the idea of being in love. Little did I realize that her and another girl in Glen Rose would be my only girlfriends until I was 33 years of age.

I said a moment ago that Michael was into his own thing. That is not exactly true. We did go down to the public pool at Oakdale Park together, swimming, and other stuff. We also did games with Mom and Dad, fairs, festivals, etc., but that youthful playing with one another, running, hide and go seek, and playing like we were members of Star Trek were pretty much over. We remained best buds but we were into all kinds of different things, some more mature.

Both of us were spreading our wings and learning to fly on our own. All of life cannot be as simple as childhood, *sad but true*. Though I'm a happy and contented older man, I sure miss this those simple, adventurous times when the world was a big place and filled with mysteries. *Ah, for the simple times*.

Anyway, Michael and I wound up getting involved in the local community theater. At the time, the members were tired of doing premade scripts and wanted something unique for Christmas. Michael wound up co-writing a script with a friend of his, Steve Bonin. They titled it, "Santa's Workshop". It was a very unique play about a bride doll who was sad because she didn't have her bridegroom.

It had a piano man, a Dumbo elephant (Michael), a puppet on strings, a ballerina, a scarecrow, and a Jack-in-the-Box (which I was). We had planned to do three performances, but as luck would have it, it was really unique and caught on like wildfire. We wound up giving performances in several places. It seems like we did it a dozen times or so to my young mind. In reality it was probably two additional performances, but I got so weary of the whole thing.

First, it became monotonous, mundane. Second, while all the rest of them were having a good time visiting socially backstage and in and around patrons of the play, I had to be buttoned down in my box in preparation for the performance. It was the fate of an actor, always doing what is best for the performance. It's not that I minded, after all, it's what I signed up for, but sometimes it would've been nice to join in on the hustle and bustle of preparation. (In reality, it was probably a case of simple envy of what the others could do. As an adult now, I don't really think it would've been better or more fun to be mill around as they did.)

I was part of the group for sure and I had, surprisingly, a good many lines for my small part. Overall, I would not exchange the experience for anything because it too was key in developing my charge forward, determined, nature.

Another thing that got me over my shyness were my parents. Mom and Dad were enablers. They supported me, in every way, to do anything I wanted. Baseball, football, tennis, cooking lessons, Cub Scouts, you name it, they were all for it. They forked over the money, their time, and skills in teaching me everything that they could as far as how to do things and mature.

3 Lifetimes In 1

In baseball, I was terrible at batting. I could field the ball pretty good, but I couldn't hit worth a flip. The first team that I was on was called Glen Lake Methodist Camp which did fairly well in the competitions. The second year I was traded to a team called Paradise Theater which wasn't so good. I played outfield on the first team, which I didn't like, and third base on the second team, which I did like.

> The irony in all this is that I got a trophy for a seventh place team on the Paradise Theater and a ribbon for a second place team for the Glen Lake Methodist Camp. Of the two, I liked that seventh place trophy out of seven teams best because I liked my teammates better and especially our manager, M. He was a down-home guy. *Very personable and friendly...*

In football, I was rough and tough and played offense and defense. I was a running back on offense that ran up the middle every time. It was not a bad position and it kept me from being overly tired because it was fairly rare that my number would be called. My main assignments were to block for the other guys.

Defense was another story altogether. If you know anything about football, our defense was a three – four, three lineman, four linebackers. I played left defensive lineman, which meant if there was a run to the left side, I was the main guy to stop it. <u>It was a while before I caught on to the fact that I had to circle around the offensive line instead of charging straight forward like a bull.</u>

Finesse is not one of my main strengths. *Charging forward where Angels fear to tread is my specialty.* About three games into the season, I finally caught on really good when the opposing quarterback circled around to my side and I had to play catch-up ball to take him down by his shoestrings.

He was really upset with me too and threw the ball right in my face. *Unfortunately, the referees didn't catch it.* The guy shouldn't have been playing anyway because he was a boy that had failed two grades and his muscular frame towered above the rest of us. Well, I came over the sidelines to talk to my Dad, who was the defensive coach. He just told me that, yes, he saw it. It was that moment that made me realize that the world is not fair and that fairness is in the eye of the beholder.

The Glen Rose High School talent show was a thing that we attended the first year more or less out of general curiosity. It was filled with things that you might expect a talent show to be made of: people playing pianos, instruments, etc. When we all saw this, we said to ourselves that next year we would give them something to remember.

We were used to doing pantomimes of Elvis, Ray Stevens, and all sorts of more lively things. It was more or less playacting for us. When you're used to doing Tina Turner's, *Nutbish City Limits*, for fun, someone playing the violin is boring. That's not to say that it doesn't take a lot of talent to do that kind of stuff, but we were used to more lively stuff with a lot of action.

So Dad got together with our friend G, who brought his best amplifiers and speakers, and we prepared to rock the house. When my Mom, Michael, and I got on stage performing a pantomime to a Ray Stevens song, *Along Came Jones*, that big auditorium came alive with laughter and applause. When Michael came out in a gold sparkling suit and did Elvis Presley's *Hound Dog*, G turned the volume way up, it is a wonder that the roof didn't come down with all the girls screaming.

It was an event to remember, for sure. When next year came, it was filled with livelier things. I remember one girl got up on stage, I think her name was K, and sang '*Take It To The Limits* by the Eagles. It was not a pantomime. She was actually singing and put Glenn Frey to shame. It was awesome!

I learned a lot just by watching her and, to tell you the truth, I was sort of envious of her talent. I suppose that's where admiration comfort comes from. You admire someone's talents because maybe you wish their abilities.

You see, at that time, I didn't think that I had any special talents of my own, unless you consider being a growing and active boy a talent. That's my youth talking because I did have many abilities. I was not very good at the rodeos that the town held, track, or much of anything else. I did excel at stereos, fishing, hunting, and spending time with my Dad, which I loved.

The first time we went to Squaw Creek, it was just me, Dad, and Mac Barnes Jr. Mac wanted to set me up with his *Mac Barnes Super Duper Hook–Up*. Now, the hookup was new to me, but Mac probably knew the area was teeming with Brim, perch, and other stuff and he probably used that to his advantage. I have to admit though, I caught a bunch of fish that day. The marvel of it all was interesting to me as I had been into magic and performed unusual close-up magic for friends and family on a regular basis.

I did the sponge ball routine, card tricks, and all sorts of other stuff. I even had a marked deck. My favorite trick was separating two large safety pins that were fastened together. I would love to tell you how it's done even though I can no longer do the trick with my own two hands, but it is a written law that a magician never reveals a trick. Trust me though, *it's fascinating*! Later on, my brother asked me to teach him the sponge ball routine and loan him the balls. Of course, I did, but hey, he's my brother.

We went to the Fort Worth zoo numerous times in addition to fairs. My Dad and I, we liked to visit the jip joints (the vendors like shooting, darts, etc.) while Mom and Michael would get on every ride that didn't ride them first. Of course, Michael and I would ride the Scrambler and other stuff. We had a blast together at every turn. We were almost inseparable. Sure, we had our own friends, but still, even in Glen Rose, our best friends were each other.

He was who I looked up to as a peer, not my friends. Oh, I had friends that I admired. I admired anyone that could achieve and were studious because Dad drilled it into my head that knowledge was power. Time and time again, *he*

3 Lifetimes In 1

would prove it. He and I built a rabbit trap from wood, set it at Squaw Creek, and caught a rabbit. When I was having trouble batting in baseball, he bought me a Johnny Bench Batter–Up.

He worked with me all summer with that thing and I hadn't hit hardly anything all season. The very last game, his construction company wanted him to go to a meeting that day. He figured missing one game wasn't a huge deal and so he talked to me and explained. I really think now that he was asking my permission (would it be okay with me?). I told him it was okay to go on and that I understood.

When it was game time, that just so happened to be the day that I hit two home runs right straight over the first baseman's head, which is exactly how he told me to hit it. He taught me how to do it and most of the credit for those two home runs goes to him for the time he spent with me.

When he got home and found out what had happened, *I was so proud to tell him about it*. He congratulated me and said that he wished he'd been there. That day haunted him until the day he died. I guess that is what taught me to make the most of today while it is here and not wait for tomorrow for anything important. Tomorrow is a figment of the imagination. There may be no tomorrow. Today is the day. Live it for right now. Live it for all your worth. Live it to its fullest. You never know what the next day is going to bring, or the next hour, or the next minute, or even the next second.

I certainly didn't.

Mark Wayne Allen

4

The End Of Life

There comes a time in everyone's life I guess that is the period from which we are changed forevermore. So it was with me, only my changing, like so many others, was a lot more radical than most.

It was the morning of September 23, 1978. My brother had visited the optometrist in the nearby town of Cleburne, Texas about a week earlier. Of course, as eye doctors always do, probably for the money, they prescribed him new glasses with a new prescription.

We were both in school at the time, so we were used to getting up early in the mornings, something I rarely ever do these days. The reason is, I am not a morning person and never have been except in school and college. I hate mornings! Maybe it's my older age or something, but at any rate, we were up that morning. It was about 8 o'clock when Michael asked me to go with him to pick up his glasses.

Well, I didn't want to go. My stomach was in knots just thinking about it. Maybe it was intuition… I don't know. Regardless, Michael followed me around the house as I got ready for the day asking, pleading, and doing everything he could to get me to go with him. It wasn't because I was afraid or didn't enjoy our time together, just a gut feeling.

Well, finally, I agreed after about an hour of this. I don't think Michael liked to be alone and I still don't think he does. When he's working on things, yes maybe, but he has asked me, when we were young, just to be in the room. Anyway, I agreed, reluctantly, to go with him even though my gut was still tied up in knots.

We took our time on the drive over there talking about old times, the present, and the future. We remembered Tink and Link, The Zink Brothers, who were "*wild and crazy guys*" (back before Steve Martin became popular).

> You see, when Mother was going to be out of the car for a moment, one of us would scoot over to the driver's seat and we pretended that the Zink Brothers were exploring, in a race, running from the law, chasing somebody, or anything like that.
>
> One day, Tink and Link were parked outside the house of a friend of Mom's and she was gone and for an exceptionally long time. Well, we were being chased by the police, gangsters, and everything else you can imagine.
>
> ## BUT...
>
> When Mom came back out and tried to start the car, <u>it was flooded</u> and wouldn't crank.
>
> She was, understandably, furious. It was a hot mid-summer day with few clouds in the sky. Mike and I were used to the heat. We stayed outside most of the time. In fact, in those days, being told to stay indoors was actually a punishment, but she, on the other hand, was not as acclimated to the heat. I have no doubt that she had better things to do besides being cooped up in a hot car waiting for it to crank.
>
> Well, after a dismal forty-five minutes, that blue Ford Maverick cranked. We were all glad to get the air-conditioning running by that time. I always liked that car though and it saddened me when it stopped running a few months later. I'm sentimental about things like that.

On with my story...

3 Lifetimes In 1

When Michael and I arrived in Cleburne in Mom and Dad's light-blue LTD Landau (Ford's biggest luxury car that Mike had borrowed for the trip), we ran in for a brand new shiny-black framed pair of glasses. They did all the fine adjustments and then we left. (*By the way, for you people that wear glasses, don't you just love the clearness of brand-new lenses, but hate getting used to them?*)

We started our journey back by, again, our usual joking and conversation. We were on the outside lane of a two-lane highway. The very last thing that I consciously remember about that morning is seeing an old beat-truck on the inside lane and Mike glancing at me and saying something. The rest of this chapter comes from testimony and police reports.

Michael began trying to merge into the one-lane going across the bridge just outside of Cleburne. When he did, the truck matched what he did and cut us off. Michael hit the brakes, of course, and tried to go behind the truck to no avail. The truck cut us off from merging so my dear brother had the choice of swerving into the truck, hitting the bridge, or going into a field.

He opted for the field.

It was a terrible situation for anyone to be in. Why these things happen, nobody knows. We were both just kids. He was 16 and I was 12. This incident was a terrible accident, more serious than most, but still just an accident. I felt harsh toward the driver of that truck for a long time, but now pray for him.

> Some people don't understand how I can be forgiving to the man who sent our whole families lives into a tailspin.

Mark Wayne Allen

> Well, people, let me tell you something. I've been through horrid physical pain that you wouldn't wish on anyone and unfathomable emotional pain. I can tell you for certain that the latter is much worse. I will let others do as they feel is right and keep on loving.

> **For all reasonable purposes, my life, as it was to be, ended on that fated morning. I'm certain that it would have been vastly different if not for "*the wreck*".**

There was an uncle that I greatly admired. He was a kinder, gentler, kind of man that had a devious side. For instance, he had a dog that all the kids were all afraid of. That is, until I came along and kicked the dog in the mouth with my cowboy boots. After spending a few minutes recovering, that dog never bothered me again.

On the flip side, you had my Grandpa who was a merchant marine captain. He was a strong figure who took no crap off of anybody. He was loud, brash, and stubborn. He wanted to be in command rather than take orders from anybody. But, he also had a sensitive, understanding side. He was very good with his hands and took total responsibility for all of his actions.

My impression is that I would have developed into a crossbreed of these two men, throw in a large dose of my Mom and Dad's good, even-tempered nature, and throw in a thirst for learning like my Dad had. Add a dash of my Mom's fun-loving, kind spirit and you've got it.

Daddy always had an expression that I never really understood until I got married. He would say that my Mom and I that could see the trees, but not the forest". Getting married changed my viewpoint. When I was living with them, my mindset was medically centered around myself. I was concerned with the immediacy of things in the world.

Marriage quickly changed my viewpoint from seeing the beauty and privilege of short-term thinking, to looking at the long term. Now, I have a similar singing. My wife sees the here and now (the trees), but I'm looking into next year and the years beyond (the forest).

> ## There is great merit to both perspectives.

"The wreck" changed everything for everyone in the family. We all had to stop and realize that everyone on this entire planet could be just a heartbeat, or a split second, away from death. Not just death, but of the life altering consequences of bad timing.

I once heard or read somewhere that the universe is only a heartbeat away from annihilation. If we turn left when we should've turned right or we get there five seconds earlier than we should, it could have deadly consequences. It went on to say that and that the entire universe was a mere five seconds away from total destruction. That's an awesome thought!

Mark Wayne Allen

Life Two

Mark Wayne Allen

5

The Next Second

Have you ever heard the expression, 'This is the first day of the rest of your life'? Well, the first day of my second life had a very rough start.

When that big LTD ran off the road, the car began to roll. On that first roll, I came out of the car or perhaps a better word would be "flew" out. Nobody talked about seatbelts in those days and very few people even used them. Some cars didn't even have them. Let that be a lesson to everyone reading this. A seatbelt would have saved a lot of heartache, misery, and pain.

> I'm sure if my Dad were alive today he would attest to that fact. He hated seatbelts, but when his truck flipped on its side, a seatbelt saved his face from being gnarled by the asphalt. It was divine protection that made him wear a seatbelt that day because he usually didn't bother.

The police estimated that I flew 50 feet in the air. When I landed, the back of my head hit a rock thereby causing unconsciousness. Can you say *instant concussion*, boys and girls? That was very fortunate indeed because on a million to one chance, that big car came down on top of me and, as you might expect, it bounced a number of times. The bouncing caused another concussion on the front of my head in the forehead region.

The wreck itself was bad enough, but to make matters worse, the catalytic converter was sitting right on top of my chest, abdomen, and the underside of the left forearm. I didn't know this about catalytic converters at the time, but it is painfully evident to me now, that **those things run very hot**. It burned into my skin and beyond.

During the incident, Michael latched onto the steering wheel and hung on for dear life. If he had not done that, who knows what would have happened to him? I am very glad that he was not physically hurt except for 17 stitches in his back from the glass that broke, but he still feels the emotional trauma of the incident to this day. I notice not from what he says or does, but he is my brother and I know him. After all, how could anyone go through that kind of ordeal and not have everlasting emotional effects?

After he recovered, he climbed out of the vehicle and looked around for me. After a few minutes, he saw my feet protruding out from underneath the vehicle. He tried to lift the car off of me and I can only imagine what kind of extreme and pervasive emotions that he was dealing with at that moment.

> They say when a person gets really excited or alarmed that their adrenaline kicks in. I can only imagine that Michael has thought about this for decades. He said that he tried to move the car. Why didn't he have enough strength? That powerless feeling of not being able to help a dearest loved one would be terrible and a terrible thing to live with. We cannot control the universe as much as we want to no matter what. That is something that I have wrestled with myself. I imagine everyone, at one time or anther, has dealt with that issue of humankind. *We are not to understand the universe, but only our small corner of knowledge.*

Soon, help arrived in the form of police and ambulances. Now here's where my story starts to be a little bit spooky. If you are a person that is rich in your faith in God, this won't come as any surprise. If you are not one of those people, these life events may be a bit hard to accept. I did not accept them at first either, but over time, the truth has been revealed to me. I can't say that I was enlightened by words, but there is truth about them and I can only hope that my writing can do justice to the things that happened and not marginalize events or feelings.

Well, they got me out from underneath the car somehow, *I don't know exactly how.* I assume it was with a wrecker or crane or wench, or something like that. The ambulance crew, which just so happened to be the best in the entire state of Texas at the time, carried me to the Cleburne Hospital. While en route, they had to revive my heart because it had stopped beating.

The staff in Cleburne immediately said that they did not have the facilities to care for such a serious burn injury so the ambulance crew began the trek to Fort Worth, Texas. My heart stopped twice more en route and was revived both times.

When they got to John Peter Smith Hospital in Fort Worth, the staff said that they didn't really didn't have the care facilities to handle such a severe burn. They recommended the burn center in Dallas, but said that I would probably not survive the extra miles. Mom and Dad told them to treat me at the hospital there rather than attempt traveling any further.

> **That was probably the choice that ended up saving my life. Weak, frail, and severely injured, there is not a doubt in my mind that I would have died during the trip.**

For all those naysayers out there that don't believe in God and Christ, there is more to my story of survival. There were two other wrecks caused by the same man that day and they were all fatal to the passengers. Because of this, help was mere minutes away because they were already mobilized. During the rolls the car made, the frame warped away from my body otherwise the catalytic converter would have been burned right through my ribs and into my chest cavity. The rope necklace that I had been wearing for about three years before that had been thrown up around my neck line and away from my chest otherwise it would have burned right through my chest.

The very first memory I had waking up was being in a small room with a clear glass wall on my right side. I was barely able to open my eyes and look at everything. I knew I was in the hospital because of all the electronic, medical gear at my sides beeping.

I had no idea what was happening or what had happened. All I knew is that I was there. Have you ever had a foggy nightmare that was so real that you thought that you could almost reach out and touch it? That's what this felt like: **a dream or nightmare that you cannot wake up from**.

I have no idea how long it had been, but every now and then people would come into the room all covered up and with masks on and as you can imagine, they would say nice things. I would drift in and out constantly it seemed like. All I knew was that I felt really bad without any idea of what was going on and so dazed that I couldn't connect one minute to the next.

<u>This was a heck of a way for a new life to start</u>. Cognitive and aware of everything, understanding what the scene was, but not being able to do much of anything because you are so weak, but with a lack of coherency. I cannot say much more about it except to say that going in and coming out of a physically tortured sleep was roughly akin to mini–death's.

That's probably not a fair and accurate description, but it's the closest that I can come. I say it that way, literally, because although I was cognitive enough to understand where I was and what was happening, I was also keenly aware, even as a 12-year-old, that the life as I knew it had ended. Nothing would ever be the same.

I knew that something catastrophic had happened. As my life before had been happy-go-lucky and doing what I wanted to such as hunting, fishing, sports, and other things, had ended. The overwhelming intensity of the emotions that I felt is even hard to write down for you, but as with all things, I adapted as best I could and tried to go along with life as it was.

3 Lifetimes In 1

After a while, how long I don't know, I became aware of family members coming in and out of the room and visiting with me. First, Mom and Daddy, always one at a time. Every now and then, my brother would come in. Different family members also came in, but whomever it was at that time, were always garbed up. Much later, I learned that I was in what they call, *reverse isolation* where everybody else insulated themselves from any reasonable means of spreading bacteria or infections to me.

I got so bored in that little room after I got to where I was not fading in and out every little while. Imagine, staring at four walls for weeks. It was an unappetizing scenario for any sensible human being. But then, something changed. My doctor, DM, finally told mom and Dad that I could eat anything that I wanted. When they first came to ask me about my first non-- hospital meal, I told them **pizza**.

Can you imagine pizza after weeks of being fed through a tube? Well, after talking about it, I decided that I would settle for a *hamburger*. The hamburger that I wanted was a quarter pounder from McDonald's and my second choice was a Jack-in-the-Box hamburger with extra special sauce. This was 10:00 A.M. in the morning.

Dad rushed right out to McDonald's and the manager told him that they were still serving breakfast so Dad explained the situation. That manager would not budge even given the situation. So, Dad turned around and went to Jack-in-the-Box. That particular manager looked at Dad, smiled, and said, "No problem, Man! How does that dude like his burger?"

So, my first solid meal after the burn was a Jack-in-the-Box hamburger with the extra special sauce. ***Can't forget the sauce***. I don't know what's in that stuff, but it is worthwhile nevertheless. YUM! I don't really hold that McDonald's manager accountable because he probably has very strict guidelines that he has to follow. You never know what individuals are going through in their lives either. We all know our station in life, but what about others. However, it would have been nice of that guy to break the rules just this once.

After that, there was a little time of visitors in and out before the doctor said that I can have anything that was battery-operated. You have to understand, that in that little room, I didn't even have a TV to gaze upon and numb my mind to the flickering of the screen. The battery order was a breakthrough so Mom and Dad went out to get every battery operated thing that money could buy. They even missed the four-hour visit rotation to do this.

> **That's something else**. I think it started out every 12 hours that I could have a visitor for 15 minutes and then I think it was every six hours and then every four hours. That's a long time in between seeing a familiar face. That's not to say that the nurses, doctors, and all weren't courteous, but *they weren't family*. They weren't loved ones. So I had all that time to myself to sleep and to wonder what else was going to come in my life. Would it be more tragedy?

3 Lifetimes In 1

There are all kinds of things that went through my mind and all kinds of fears, a lot too horrible to mention. I was trying my best to recover and go on the best way that I could, but life and even time was uncertain minus those 15 minute intervals with family trying to tell you what all has happened and then trying to reassure you that all is going to be okay.

Yes, I was a 12-year-old-year-old kid who was trying to get on with life as best I could, but in the back of my mind, I always knew things were not simply going to go back to the way used to be. Endless doubts emerged. Directo**r John Carpenter** was once asked why there were no graphic kill scenes in the movie *Halloween*. His reply was that there was nothing that he could put on-screen as scary as what a person's mind could imagine. Well, friends, I can tell you that his statement is very true.

We were all trying to deal with the crisis as best we could. *This I am sure of.* I'm positive that everyone was in shock. My brother was probably replaying our wreck in his mind 10,000 times per day wondering if he had done something different would it have made the outcome any better. My Dad would was probably drowning in his own pain as much as anybody, after all, it was he and I that had palled around doing outdoor stuff most of the time.

And my poor Mother was so pulled into herself that she grabbed the only tangible thing that she could hold onto, my rope necklace. She was in so much emotional pain that that simple gold rope necklace was directly linked to my life.

She imagined that as long as she held on to that necklace, that I would live.

She had it in her hands for weeks and then dropped it one night while sleeping. Waking up the next morning, my dear Mother was in a frenzied panic. She began clamoring over everything that was near to her, underneath, on top, to the sides, with stark terror. To and fro she went and when she regained possession of that necklace, it went straight into her hand.

Different people had tried to hold the necklace for her, but she would not give it up. I can't say as I blame her. It's unclear as to what point Mother decided that holding onto my necklace ceased as a priority, but I imagine it was after I was out of the intensive care unit.

Michael, along with everybody else, was filled with worry about his little brother I'm sure. I can only try to imagine what horrible agony everyone went through. I have all ideas that it was as difficult for them mentally as it was for me physically. Not one of us would ever be the same after this tragedy.

One thing I forgot to mention. Shortly after I was admitted to John Peter Smith Hospital, they had a blood shortage. Well, word had already gotten back to the Brown & Root jobsite where my Dad worked. Now, at that particular jobsite, my Dad, George W. Allen, was a general foreman of welding and had about 600 people working under him. The entire jobsite consisted of, I don't know the exact figure, but I imagine it was well over 2000 men and women.

> When those people heard that I needed blood, the very next day, over 400 construction workers showed up at the hospital to give blood. The hospital didn't even have an accurate count of just how many people it was because they started turning people away. They simply couldn't accommodate all of them.
>
> *That is an awesome thought*. A lot of those people knew me and some of them knew me on a personal level. Those that didn't, knew my Dad and some people showed up because they knew only there was a need of a company employee or family member. The outpouring of graciousness makes my heart swell with pride to this very day. The tenderness of people to allow themselves to be touched and to serve the community where there is a known need really makes me feel warm with good emotions. <u>It shows off the best in humanity as a species</u>.
>
> Brown & Root employees is, or was, a tight-knit group. They are like a big family. It was a pleasure and privilege to know them all.

Before long, it was time to start healing and to do that meant cleaning the burn. Unfortunately, that meant the standard whirlpool baths to clean the area. I can still remember the trip down to my first whirlpool bath. I remember that like it was yesterday because of the events that followed.

Well, I saw the bathtub there beside me and I remember being anxious. My anxiety rose when they removed the bandages that were covering the burn. This was the first time that I ever actually saw the damaged area.

There was pink flesh everywhere and I remember how big of an area it was. There were no scabs or puss, but pitted pink flesh glimmered in the bright fluorescent lights of the room. I remember my muscles starting to quiver and my mind thinking how wrong this was. The more I looked at naked injury, the more reality burned into my mind the severity of my demise. I was just a 12-year-old child back then and like many other youths that were fated to similar circumstances, I was not ready for any of this. Who is?

I trembled at the idea of being bathed in the aerated water in the metal tub beside me and it escalated when that hoist started to lift me up. Slowly, but surely, the staff maneuvered me over the tub, then lowering into the water. My Mom was at my side the whole time and was trying to keep me calm by saying reassuring things like how good the water would feel. I give her credit, as well as the lab technician, for doing their best, but when that water started touching the burned area, it caused great pain that I can only describe ***through the roof***.

"Through the roof" is an under exaggeration. Please understand, I have a very high tolerance for pain of any type and always have had.

I have tried to describe the pain myself to other people many times, but my descriptions always fall short. Suffice it to say that it is the only times in my life, before or after the wreck, that I honestly and truly wished I was dead rather than having to go through that pain. I'm talking about searing pain that is all encompassing and that you can't get away from, turn off, or do anything about. As a kid, I didn't know how long it would last. If Hell is worse than this, <u>and I'm positive that it is</u>, I would suffer many deaths.

Regardless of how long it lasted. ONE SECOND of that kind of pain is too much. I am talking about burns that were so deep that you could see, with the naked eye, two of my rib bones. That whirlpool bath might as well have been in boiling water for the pain that I was feeling (*I'm sure the water was lukewarm*).

I know it must have been impossibly difficult for my Mother to see me in such a state. I was screaming. I was hollering. I was saying, "get me out", " I wish I was dead", and similar such things. I think the whirlpool bath lasted 20 minutes, but I can't be sure right now. Whatever length of time it was, it was too long and seemed like an eternity to me.

Well, we were through with the first one. The next one came a few days after. My Mom, bless her heart was hurting so much from the struggle of getting me through the first one asked the doctor to come in on the second.

On my way down the hall going to the whirlpool bath, I felt like a prisoner of war being sent to a torture chamber. The people around me were lighted-hearted and supportive, but my mind knew that bath was required and my body was itching to revolt. If it could've, I truly think it would've ran away, but it was not to be.

I was cringing from very moment the bath was mentioned, but was at relative ease with everything until I was in that room. All of us have experienced a situation where we knew something had to be done, but we didn't want to do it. Well, I knew this had to be done, what it was for, and that there was no way to remove myself from the situation. That having been said, *I was truly terrified.*

Words cannot illustrate how painful it was to be in that water. In hindsight, there might have been something about actually seeing the burned area in the bubbling water that was circulating around me... Visuals work upon the mind and manifest themselves physically and emotionally also. I really don't think that the sight of the burn had all that much to do with it, but there's always a chance that I could be wrong.

I was young, immature, and to be honest with you, I don't think I could really grasp the depth and scope of what was going on at my age. *But…* I grew up fast! My childhood was ended at the time of the wreck. *It's a pity.* All young kids should have that youthful innocence prolonged as long as possible. There's something magical about those times. Unfortunately, I was among the many young people all over the country whose childhood ended quickly. **Heck, forget country**: the world.

Kids contract cancer just the same as adults do. In most cities all over the world, even here in the United States, children have to grow up on the streets and survive however they can. There are kids overseas that have to fight for food, clothing, and shelter. I just think it's a shame that any kid should have to go through that, least of all medical illness.

Well, at my Mom's insistence, the doctor observed my second whirlpool bath at some time or other. I say that because I only have people's word that he did because I didn't see him. *What was his reaction*? He told everyone to get me out of there because he was afraid that I would go back into shock. **Yes, it was that severe**!

He said that we would handle it surgically. In other words, by putting me to sleep every time. He said that there was a little more risk involved but it was better than the alternative.

I tell you, it was such a relief to hear about the news!!!!!!!!!!!! I just cannot tell you how gleeful I was!!!!!!!!!!

Although 38 years has passed since that time, I can still remember those whirlpool baths just like they were yesterday. **I never will forget them**. Since those baths, there have been frequent times that I could remember that searing pain turning like a knife in my skull like it happened yesterday.

To truly be honest with you, I don't know how the human body can endure severe pain like that. Compared to all other pains I've ever had in my life, nothing even comes close, and I've had some really intense experiences. It's impossible to conceptualize, but take the most sharp, searing pain that you've ever experienced and multiply it times ten million. That may come close.

> Michael turned 17 while I was in the hospital. We had a birthday party for him in my room. I don't remember where him and his friend A, who was at the event with us, were headed that night but it was all in celebration of his birthday. I am overjoyed that he got to do some fun stuff while I was cooped up in that hospital room. I hope the pair went someplace special. I was all smiles that evening.
>
> In retrospect, life must have been hard for Michael to go to school and proceed with daily living with everyone constantly asking questions. What happened? How is your brother? What is the latest news? Any sane person would get tired of answering the same questions over and over again and I imagine that forced him to think about the event much more than he wanted to.
>
> I can only imagine how life continued for him as I have only been in similar circumstances less than a handful of fingers and then only for a few days at a time, certainly a manageable number. There's a big difference in how you handle each situation. For them life slowed to a painful crawl mentally.

There was a student nurse that we dealt with. The first day that she came and talked to us, she said that she was doing a final paper and in order to graduate, but it in order to do the paper, she had to do like a case study on someone. Well, Mother and I talked about it and decided if my situation could ever help someone, then we wanted it to. So, she, practically speaking, moved in with us.

She was a very nice woman and she helped us out in every aspect that you can imagine. A very welcome relief to a bunch of weary souls... She would often write into a spiral notebook. This was her log of our case. She stayed with us for almost a month, I think, and I really wish that I could remember her name, but I can't. *Maybe someday* I will remember.

You never know what form Angels will take. Mom was in the hospital nearly at all times with me. Michael and Daddy were there a lot too, but it was mainly Mom doing the bulk of things. God sent his Angel down to help us rest, cope, and have a brief rest from the daily drudgery.

My left arm had a partial cast that inhibited movement. During my surgeries for cleaning the burned area, the doc said he worked my arm vigorously to keep it from freezing up, thus avoiding great difficulty working it loose again in the therapy that was to come later. That effort alone probably saved a month or more in therapy. (*another blessing*)

I went through many surgeries during my hospital stay. I was always friendly to the staff in the O.R., but I must digress for a moment. They would roll me down to surgical waiting and after a few times of asking questions, I knew which drugs I liked best, which needles were least painful, what tubing they needed, and so to infinity.

And let me tell you, of all my 30+ surgeries to date (some more severe than others), I can safely tell you that surgical nurses are the wackiest bunch of people that you will ever meet. <u>I say that with the greatest affection</u>. Their job is sometimes tragic and I certainly wouldn't want it.

Coming out of surgery was bad, especially when they took skin off the backs of my legs. That particular morning, Dr. M was delayed and another doctor started the operation. I will always believe he cut too deep because some areas developed thicker scars.

When I woke up in recovery, I stayed in agonized, writhing pain nearly the whole time I was there. They gave me as much pain medication as they could, then simply gave up trying. You see, although I could barely talk, it was the nerve endings causing the pain. That is the toughest kind of pain to treat and I learned much later that there was not anything that could be done for the pain itself (at that time at least).

3 Lifetimes In 1

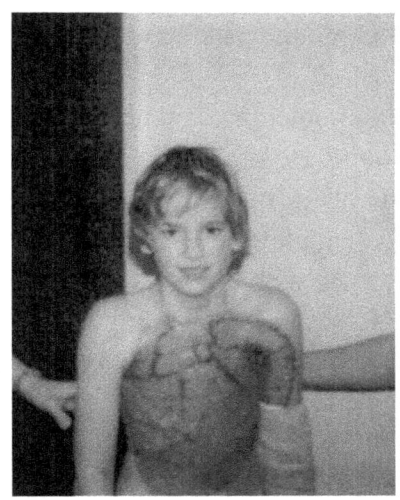

Now my Dad had been a Dallas Cowboys fan ever since the football franchise was founded. He followed them as they built up from a weakling team to a major powerhouse under the guidance of Tom Landry. Now every football fan knows who Tom Landry was, but if you don't recognize the name, he was the first ever coach of the Dallas Cowboys and the winningest coach ever in NFL football history. He is in the NFL Hall of Fame now in Canton, Ohio.

Several years after the franchise was formed, the Dallas Cowboys went to the Super Bowl for two years in a row and lost both times. The next season, they ended up going to the Super Bowl again. Dad made every bet that he could. These were funds that they didn't actually have. "**IF**" the Dallas Cowboys were to lose, they would have to borrow money to cover the bets. He never remembered how much he actually did bet, but he just knew that it was more money than they had.

Coming home one day, he finally decided to tell Mom what he had done. He figured he would get a lecture and a scolding on the value of money. My Dear, Sweet, Mom, was not into football at all until she married my Dad. She only got into the sport to be with him and talk on his level about the intricacies of football. She got into it too much maybe?

When she learned what he'd done, she looked at him with her eyes wide open and told him to go bet another hundred for her. *Is that trust or what???* I'm not really sure how to classify it myself. *Was it faith in him, the team, or what???*

Regardless, he never did collect on all the debts when the Dallas Cowboys won.

Now, when I was younger, I hated and despised football. I even threatened to bash the TV screen in with a bat so no one could watch them play. I was disposed to acting like a pistol, always shooting off like that. (I kind of think that's how I ended up standing too close and peeing on a gas heater. It scalded my *woo hoo*, but that's another story.)

Anyway, for better or worse, I grew up with the Dallas Cowboys being on all of the TV screen's every season, all season long. When we moved to Glen Rose, Texas, some Dallas Cowboy games were not being carried on the local networks.

3 Lifetimes In 1

> You see, the NFL has a policy, or did up until the 2015 season, that if you lived within 100 miles of the stadium in which the game was played and the game was not a sellout, then there was a mandatory local TV blackout.
>
> But you see, a true NFL fan will do most anything to see their team play. My Dad and four of his buddies, I think, decided that there was a station in Waco that that was out of the blackout zone and carried the games all the time. So, Dad bought extension poles and boosted our aerial antenna from about 50 feet to 300 feet up in the air. (*There was no such thing as cable TV back then.*)
>
> Normally, two-inch aluminum poles would not stand up that tall on their own, but Dad dealt with all kinds of metal on a daily basis and knew this. He attached four quarter-inch steel cables to the pole of the antenna as guide wires. When we had to pick up Waco, somebody had to stay indoors and watch the TV while somebody went outdoors and turned that immense antenna towards Waco. It was such a sight!

I was gone for a while on a tangent, but now I'll tell you what I was aiming to. Like I say, we were all Dallas Cowboys fans at that time, me included, so my Dad called their front office and was going to try and get a card signed by the team or something. Well, the person that he talked to said they could do a little better than that. He was to just wait for a call back after that person talked with the managers. Anyway, next thing you know, the then backup quarterback Danny White and a defensive player (*the name of which escapes the entire family*) visited me in John Peter Smith Hospital.

I will never forget their visit. They stayed over an hour and a half visiting with all of us. The defensive guy kind wasn't very talkative, either by design or accident, and Danny was the most unrestrained with his words and manners. He was a Christian man that talked about absolutely everything that he or we could think of. He even let us hold his Super Bowl ring, which was amazingly heavy and shiny. It was white gold encrusted with diamonds.

At the end of their visit, Danny took out a simple black and white publicity photo of himself on a football field fading back to pass. On it, he took out a pen and scribbled some writing on it. When I was handed the gift and turned it, the inscription read, 'Work hard, pray hard, and **NEVER** give up!!!' The word never was underscored three times and at the bottom was his signature. That simple publicity photo and message we put in a gold frame made of aluminum, tin, or something like that.

That photo is still hanging on my wall today. It has guided me through many tough times. I thank God for Danny's presence in my life at that time and beyond. I think of him often. I actually caught up with him on Facebook about a year ago and told him how much of an inspiration he was to me. After about a month, he replied and told me that he was glad that he could be a positive influence.

I would be held in contempt if I didn't mention a family friend named Larry. I think of him more as extended family now for all that we've been through in all three of my lifetimes.

Everybody in the family became weary at points. Staying at a hospital with me for hours, days, and months on end would get tiring to anybody. It's understandable. I went in the hospital about mid-August and was not expected to get out until sometime in January.

Sometimes I needed more or less, but by the time you add daily eating, drinking, bathroom breaks, etc., it made for a lot to do. Well, Larry would step in and take his turn spending the night with me. Now, I had a urinal at my bedside that I wee wee'd in and Larry told me that he didn't care if it was full, if I couldn't wake him needing something, *'throw that thing.'*

He never failed to wake up in an instant.

By the time that I finally got out of the hospital, I had been through nineteen surgeries, but even after I got out, there was still work to be done in the form of physical therapy. You see, under my left arm was a tight band, kind of like a webbing, which was where the skin melted and sagged. They thought that this band could be worked out, or rather stretched out, during therapy.

I would try to stretch it out with weights after soaking my scars in hot paraffin wax, which was kind of oily. But one day, I was trying to stretch it out, and blood gushed from where the skin had ripped. We spent at least the next half-hour trying to get it to stop. That evidently was a sign to the therapist that we were not going to be able to stretch it out. So, she recommended another surgery.

Now at the same time, I had been going to homebound school trying to catch up with where the other kids were. The state of Texas, at the time, was number one scholastically and I was falling far, far behind my classmates. I thought, at the time, that I'd be able to catch up given a reasonable chance, but age and maturity has convinced me that that notion was unrealistic.

Missing three months of classes in a school system like that was probably far too much. It would've taken a long time for me to catch up. So, it was recommended, I don't know by who, that I might have a better chance of catching up in another state that was ranked lower.

Well, one thing led to the other, and since my Dad was in construction, moving was always an option and there just happened to be a job opening in Ashdown, Arkansas. So, we, yet again, loaded up our belongings in Glen Rose, Texas, and would move. I was in no shape to help anyone, so Mom and I headed to Shreveport, Louisiana and met with a plastic surgeon, whose name I can't recall, about giving me some help. We scheduled surgery for two weeks later I think and headed back to Texas to help with the packing as best we could.

Let me inject this note about moving. Everybody around our house always hated it because the whole house was psychologically and deliberately manipulated into a war zone.

Mom was a meticulous packer. She would painstakingly wrap every little knickknack that we had ever bought, sorted through everything, and wind up throwing away at least some of the stuff. She considered every little piece that we had collected in our travels and vacations and what have you to be a precious gems worthy of cherished protection. Following her philosophy, we would've had to pack at least two months prior to actual loading the stuff and getting on the road.

Did I say "two months"??? **I meant to say more like six months**.

Now we come to Daddy whose philosophy was to get it in the truck and get on with the show. Now, some stuff may get damaged, but that's the way the ball bounces. As long as we got to where we were headed safely and as soundly with at least 80% of our stuff undamaged, that was a successful trip.

I trust that you can easily see how these two philosophies mix together about as good as fire and gasoline. Take this scenario and mix in two kids and you have yourself a good nitroglycerin bowling alley mixed in with a few flaming darts just for fun. The best thing Michael and I learned how to do was to keep our heads low and our mouths shut.

That's not easy to do when you have to ask, and answer, questions. I am reminded of a quote by Winston Churchill who said, "*Speak softly and carry a big stick*," only we tried to do the first part only, "*Speak softly*". The whole house was turned completely upside down and everybody was in the firing line. Dad would take things out of the truck and a little while later Mom would ask about that box. Then, naturally, we would say that it was already packed and then Mount MOM would erupt. What's more, she would go to look for something and Dad would say that he found a half-packed box so he stuffed the item that she needed to fill the box up. He subsequently loaded it into the truck.

Mount MOM again! Mount DADDY would appear at this point because how was he to know… Worse yet, Daddy would say, "*Boys, go load this in the truck.*" If we were to say anything back other than "*yes, sir*", we would be accused of being disrespectful and get in trouble. We were always taught if one parent told us something, then don't go asking the other, so it was damned if you do and damned if you don't. *There was no way to win.* The best we could do was to keep our heads low and not do anything. Then, we would get in trouble for not helping out. If we did anything, there was a chance it was wrong. *For us kids*, there was no way to win.

After two weeks of packing and loading, Michael and Dad headed to Ashdown while Mom and I headed to Shreveport for my surgery. As I've indicated before, I was an inquisitive young boy and whenever I would be headed to surgery, I would ask 39,000 different questions. I would ask about the drugs, the lights, the gloves, and everything else. By the time that I was headed for this surgery, I knew what drugs

3 Lifetimes In 1

I wanted, what needles I wanted, where I wanted them, what bags I wanted, where I wanted them at, and everything else you can imagine.

This would be my 20th surgery and, when it was all over, that doctor told my Mom that I knew more about that operating room than some of the people that were working in there.

I was making sure that I knew everything about it because I had been told that I would need at least one surgery per year to expand the grafted tissue to allow for my growth. You see, scar tissue, which is what the grafted tissue is, does not grow as fast as normal tissue. (*Thankfully, I never had to have a "release" surgery. I wouldn't want to go through that pain anyway.*)

I nearly begged that plastic surgeon not to do a skin graft when he cut out that band of skin although, he almost guaranteed me he would have to do that. (*The pain, the pain...*)There's a little known fact about skin grafting: the donor sites are equivalent to a second-degree burn.

My burn was certainly a large area to graft skin. They had to take the donor skin from my abdomen, front, back (as mentioned earlier), and sides of my thighs. There is no way to describe the searing pain that ensued from the removal of the skin. I didn't explained this before but what they do is to take an extremely thin blade and remove only the surface layer of skin. Of course, I was asleep on the operating table for this procedure, but waking up with that overwhelming pain was a real trip.

I'm talking about an all-encompassing, barely able to breathe, mind blowing type of pain that resonates down to the very spirit and core of your mind, body, and soul. If it were an earthquake, it would easily be a 15 on the Richter Scale. Having the burn was mind blowing enough, but to have the skin grafting on top of that added immensely to a deepening of pain that would be forever seared into my memory.

> **As bad as it was, it didn't even come close to the pain from the whirlpool baths.**

*** That was beyond bearable!!!! ***

I talked to several psychologists before being released from John Peter Smith Hospital that were concerned about my mental well-being. They said I was okay. Looking back on it, I don't know how a person could ever think that I would ever be totally, for lack of a better word, balanced.

I knew I wasn't okay even while I was talking to them. What else did they think that I was going to do? If life gives you something that's bad, what else can you do but try to make the best of it. The idiocy of trying to assess if I was traumatized is laughable.

6

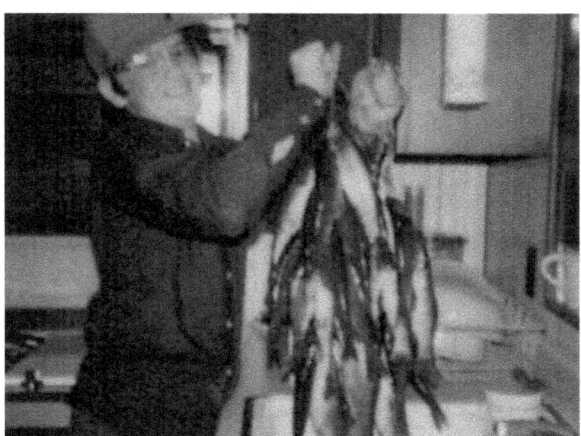

Breaking A Person

After having my life totally shattered, Hell No! I was not okay. Before the wreck, I was an athletic, sports-minded, physically active, extremely outgoing person that always had dogs, rabbits, and anything else around me. I was a lover of football, baseball, soccer, tennis, and just about everything else that you can think of and more.

Let me explain something here. Skin grafts are paper thin and highly subject to damage. Once damage happens, the skin, being scar tissue, heals extremely slowly. I was told by doctors that I couldn't play sports or have pets. They even cautioned me against running. They were saying all this to me as a young child of 12 years old probably not realizing the mental effects. The grafted skin was only one layer of tissue. *One!!!* It is tissue paper thin.

I had to wear a Jobst vest each day because grafted tissue is like any other scar tissue on your body, it has a tendency to build up, especially around the edges. The vest acted like sandpaper and files down the skin thus reducing this build up. Unfortunately, it is hot and hard to put on. And as you can figure, it was almost another layer of skin. <u>Very tight</u>!!!

Allow me to explain something else while I'm at it. My Dad, and my Mom also, I guess, in their efforts to protect me from the emotional distress of being in the courtroom with the so-and-so who drove us off the road kind of isolated me from not having to go into the courtroom and face this guy.

I agree that it would've been a really, really bad scene, probably all the way around, but in my mind, I was looking anxiously forward to telling that man exactly what I thought of him. Mind you, I'm being straight-forward and honest about the situation. It truly would've been a tumultuous scene, complete with frenzied outbursts, had I been allowed in the courtroom with that scuzzball, and, in fact, I know would have. It would've been very bad for all concerned, including myself, but I never got the emotional release.

I had a lot of pinned up anger towards that guy. Since that time, I've dealt with the emotions better and now feel sorry for him. You see, over the years I've learned from the school of life that he's had to live with the knowledge that he, not only caused our wreck, but a number of fatalities that day.

3 Lifetimes In 1

Anyway, it is what it is, and my confronting him in court wouldn't have made a difference in the outcome of my life anyway. I say outcome, but I am not dead yet, so that is probably not an accurate way of describing it. At least I hope I'm not dead yet. If I am, all this work would have been for naught. Ha!

> If you've ever studied phenomenology you know that everything we really know about the world is relayed to us through our senses and that we really have no knowledge about the world around us. We only trust our senses with no real way of knowing if they are giving us correct information. It's an interesting concept that I just thought I'd mention.

Anyway, I was very worried about myself and my condition. It necessitated an entire rethinking of how I approached life. Instead of being a charge forward, take the bull by the horns and do what is physically and emotionally called for kind of guy, I felt like I was forced into living what my body claimed was necessary, a very reserved, quiet, and limited person.

I wanted a pet of some sort so I was able to get a hamster which the doctors told me that I could have. He was average size with the typical white spot on the right side of his back. Marmaduke bit me every chance that he got, but I have to admit that, as a typical young teenager, I would take him out to play with him without washing my hands or anything.

Mark Wayne Allen

As you can figure, I probably had yummy, smelly food on my hands each time. You know, you can't spank a hamster or even punish them with any efficiency, although I tried. I used his food as bait to try to lure him into behaving correctly. Of course, it didn't work. He didn't bite me every time though.

He was a good companion that would travel around the house inside his plastic ball.

I don't really remember too much about Arkansas except that we went fishing quite a bit. We always found fishing from the bank to be easier and we had this one spot that we would go down to nearly every evening. We had this honey hole that we would always try to cast into. Unfortunately, there was a tree in the water that was beside the spot and limbs over it.

As you can imagine, we had great difficulty casting into that exact spot. About every third time, we would end up casting into the tree instead of the water. Sometimes we could coax the line out, but more often than not, we would end up having to pull and break a line. (and it was not unusual to hit the tree trunk either) *Yeah, those flying fish were elusive. Ha!*

I don't think anyone fished in that spot but us. By the time we left, approximately 6 months later, I bet there was about $100 of fishing tackle stuck in that tree.

The other thing I remember about Arkansas, other than being extremely self-conscious about my burns and grafted tissue was being in the band. You see, I had started playing trumpet in Glen Rose for about a year and two months. My first year was under Mr. MC who had just been hired for us beginners.

He was awesome! Probably in hindsight, he was aiming for the high school band director's position all along. He evidently saw something in my playing and had me as his first chair. As a beginner band, we were doing musical pieces that quasi-rivaled what the high school band was doing under Mr. P. Halfway through the year, Mr. MC pulled me and a friend of mine (saxophone) aside after class and told us that he wanted to work with us one-on-one to introduce a musical piece to the rest of the class for our final performance of the year.

Well, after a while, I don't know how long, we performed it for the entire band and <u>it was awesome</u>, if I don't mind saying so myself. From that miniature performance, we started rehearsing the whole song as a group effort. That's how I spent the final weeks of the school year. *I loved it!* I thought the song was great and I loved playing the trumpet. **Heaven!**

Few things have ever brought me as much joy as blowing my horn. I really had a passion for it. Of course, that would later become a moot point.

The next school year, Mr. MC got a well-deserved promotion to the high school band and, regrettably, we got Mr. P whose idea of an up-tempo song was the *Blue Danube Waltz.*

I say all this to tell you that the only thing I didn't miss about moving away is Mr. P. In Arkansas, there was an outstanding band director. He was the definition of charisma and I have tried and tried to remember his name down through the years, but the name escapes me. Our final performance of the year was a rock 'n roll medley at the start of which we all put on dark sunglasses and teetered while we played.

Now that's what I call a band director!

We had only been living in Ashdown Arkansas for about six months when Mom and Dad decided that we were moving to Alabama. Now there's a little something that I left out about the place we had moved into. It was a home, yes, but it was over an abandoned convenience store. Dad and Michael had had the privilege of moving us in by themselves as Mom and I were getting my plastic surgery. In the meantime, since Michael had been in the schools of Glen Rose for about four years, Mom and Dad had let him stay there and finish high school with his friends. Which, I'm glad he got the opportunity to do.

It was after his graduation that we moved from Arkansas to Milbrook, Alabama. This was right after the trucker's strike back in the late 1970's and my Mom always had a fear of running out of food. Well, as you can imagine, she had just had two weeks before, bought every scrap of canned goods that she could lay her hands on. I think she

3 Lifetimes In 1

must have got things that we didn't even eat like artichokes and pickled pig hearts.

As you can imagine, that entire upstairs house was packed so much with food that it should've toppled over. To make matters worse, we had a huge chest-type freezer that she so very carefully packed with, yep, you guessed it, canned goods. Four grown men with a dolly couldn't even budge the thing.

We ended up having to unpack the freezer, boxing the cans, and then carting everything downstairs. There were exactly 26 steps on the staircase. You might ask me how I remember this? Because friends, we all made several hundred trips up and down them moving out of that place.

Oh, before I forget, I need to mention a great thing that my brother did. We were coming back home one day and I had gotten mad at him for some reason or other. The reason is totally beside the point now. Now there was a local radio station that was located on the road to home from Ashdown.

I wouldn't even talk to Mike much that day so he stopped at the radio station, invited me to come in with him. Of course, I was stubborn and said no. Well, he came back in a few minutes and we were once again on our way.

In a few minutes the song, 'Soul Man' by the Blues Brothers started playing with the announcer saying something about it sounded like a lovers spat to him. I immediately recognized the song and accepted it as an apology.

The only thing in the song that could possibly sound like a lovers quarrel to us was it indicated something about a boyfriend. Ha! Little did they know. My Dad was always fond of the saying, 'We were just making memories.' Memories are sometimes good, sometimes bad, but time eventually makes them all softer and easier to handle.

> If that weren't true, I wouldn't be here. Be that as it may, we've made a lot of memories and of the ones created by us instead of circumstance, they are mostly good.

With the U-Haul all packed up, we set out for Millbrook, Alabama. Dad rented us a very nice house, complete with a fenced in yard. Michael decided after a short while to get his own place and I, again, was in another school.

Again, I did not make many friends. In Arkansas, I was very much introverted. Alabama was not much better. I was in eighth grade and hated it. I didn't like my peers and made a handful of friends.

The music of playing my trumpet that had kept me going in Arkansas under an outstanding band director was watered down under Mr. F. At first, he wanted me to join the high school band and play a horn that I had never played before: a flugelhorn.

Well, in the simplest of terms, I was not ready. The high school band had been playing together for at least two weeks before school even started. Between that, trying to learn the steps on the football field, and trying to blow in a

3 Lifetimes In 1

new horn which was bigger than I was used to, was just too much for me at that point.

I was not mentally ready either. Expecting me to take initiative when I was just trying to get myself oriented in a new town and to pull myself up from the mentally reserved pit that I was in was too much. *(Like they say, hindsight is 20/20. I didn't realize ANY of this at the time.)*

After about a week, Mr. F switched me to the junior high band, or as they called it, the little band. I liked that much better. First of all, it was sit down and play like I was used to and, additionally, it was popular sounds like, "Get Up And Boogie" and the "The Candy Man". I loved playing that music!

A breakthrough event in my life was when it was finally decided that I could have a dog. Mom and I went to the local pound and I picked out a mixed-breed (we called them Heinz 57's) and brought him home. He looked like a mix of Daschund (long body), Poodle (blackish curled hair), and had the manner of a Hound (he gulped food), and was very lovable.

He was cute! He was a fish dog. We caught fish, threw it up on the bank, and Snuffy (short for Sesame Street's Mr. Snuffleupagus), would dig a hole, and put the fish in it. If it flopped out, he'd put it back in.

In my mind, Snuffy was a sense of normalcy. Things were leveling out, although I knew my physical state was a permanent one.

Like I sad, I did not make many friends. I found it hard to break out of my protective shell with all that I had been told about my physical being. Psychologically, I guess I was protecting myself physically and emotionally from anything and everything by not developing attachments.

<u>Regardless, it was much better to have been informed of everything</u>, but it was such a harsh break from my former lifestyle, that it was a big adjustment. Starting in Alabama, when I was alone at night, I would tear up. I'm not sure why, but in hindsight, I think I the tearing was an attempt to relieve stress from the burn.

In the hospital, the immediate goal was physical healing. I adapted the best way I knew how. I never realized the magnitude of what I was dealing with. *How could I?*

Alabama did have one redeeming asset. After a short time, G, the guy that gave me the stereo in Glen Rose, moved to town. When he did, he brought a gift for me, a control-line gas-engine airplane. If you've never seen the things, they are awesome! You fill the gas tank up, stand in the center of an area with the controller in your hand that operates the elevators and go round and round until the engine runs out of gas.

Now that I think about it in those terms, it sounds kind of dumb, but to a young kid who was a hobbyist, this was great fun! The plane was a P-51 Mustang, silver, and boy she was beautiful. Every Saturday we would go out and fly planes on the school grounds. There was a perfect place between three buildings that sheltered us from the wind, or at least partly.

When we would get back, we would all sit around the table with Mom and Dad talking about the morning's adventures and just general chit-chat. Well, one Friday night, Dad told me not to go with G the next morning. I didn't understand at all because I felt like that was my relief from the week's turmoil at school. A, a friend of Mike's, was staying with us at the time and he tried to talk to me while G and his wife were parked outside our house the next morning waiting on me to come out. I didn't understand the full impact of what he was saying right then, but looking back on it, I do. He was trying to tell me that Mom and Dad needed a break from the same old routine and people. Anyone, it may be your best friend in the whole world, can get tiring if you see them often enough.

The next week, I went out with G again and flew planes. The hiatus was merely a temporary reprieve for the household.

We went fishing a lot in Alabama too and we were always losing fishing tackle to the flying fish, i.e. tree branches. So I said enough was enough and put a plastic bucket in the middle of the yard and tied a rubber weight on the end of my line. After casting into that bucket from different positions about 10,000 times, I got pretty good at

> casting and hitting the mark that I wanted. The next time we went fishing, I was casting for Mom too at times.

Mentally and Emotionally, I was struggling to keep my head above water. Every day seemed like a weight that was constantly drifting my attention and making me depressed. I can tell you all this, because hindsight is 20/20. Although I was having fun a lot of time, it just seemed like I was struggling for concentration at others. I needed self-consistency and wasn't ale to achieve it. My thoughts would often wander to the bad times at John Peter Smith Hospital. Loud noises or anything that was sudden seemed to catch me off balance. It was nothing major mind you and not even enough to talk about with anyone because it was so sporadic, but still it was going on.

After six months of living in Alabama, it was time to move again. Such is the construction life. This time we were off to Wyoming. Green River to be exact... Getting up there proved to be a challenge.

We rented a U-Haul trailer and prepared to move up to Wyoming in February. Dad had tried to hire a moving company, but no one would move us up there during the winter. We would soon find out why.

After we were packed and ready to go, we took off and headed to Dumas, Texas, where we spent the night. The next morning, we set out at first light like we usually do. Although there was a snowstorm, we were still headed out.

3 Lifetimes In 1

Not even 5 miles out of town that U-Haul trailer was sliding all over the road because of the wind, so we went back to Dumas and spent another night. The next morning we tried again and the trailer was slipping and sliding all over the road because of the ice and wind, so we headed back and spent another night. The next morning when we headed out, the same thing happened: shipping and sliding all over the road.

Dad was afraid of winding up in a ditch somewhere and that's probably exactly what would've happened had we not turned back each time. Since we knew that we couldn't find a moving company that would move us up there in February, he found one that would bring our stuff to us in June. We found a storage place and I guess Dad paid in advance for the extra three months so and we set out again the next day, just us, the few belongings that we need to survive in the interim, and the car.

When we got there, we found ourselves living in a makeshift trailer park. I say makeshift because there were numerous other trailers around us about 6-feet from each other on three sides. Brown & Root, which was the company that hired Dad to come up there, promised him a fine house for us to live in, complete with yard, and other accouterments.

They told him that it was temporary while the real housing facilities were being built. We lived in that small trailer with makeshift curtains, none of our stuff, and, as you can imagine, it was very droll. It felt almost like when my wife and I were displaced by Hurricane Rita. If you've never been evacuated or displaced by anything, just imagine ripping yourself up by force and moving into a hotel, having to buy groceries and the needful things such as toiletries, food, and the like, while you don't know how long it is that you'll be staying at your present location. It's an unsettling thing that rocks you down to your core.

Kelley and I stayed with a friend during our evacuation, which was a blessing and an act of generosity that I will never forget. The courtesy of Ed was amazing. He turned his home into our home. That kind of person deserves a lot of credit and thankfulness. He only knew us through my brother and a little bit of collaborative work between he and I which is not really enough, you would think, for a person to open their home. Ed is truly a dear friend and fellow Christian.

> Telling you this, I cannot help but think about the people that were in New Orleans when Katrina hit. Granted, they had been told to evacuate, but chose to stay. How terrible of a tragedy that entire fiasco was and there is enough fault for everyone to have some, but the fact remains that when it was all done, the survivors that stayed in New Orleans ended up in a terrible situation, totally displaced from everything that they knew.

Back in Wyoming, after about a week or two of the trailer, my Dad said parenthetically, 'By gosh that's enough!' I am reminded here about General George S Patton whose temper was only equaled by his skill as a war soldier. When Dad had had enough, *something had to give*. You didn't want to get in his way when he was on a mission because he would knock you down like a bowling pin, at least verbally.

You'd know that you got scolded, like a kid with their hand in the cookie jar, but so warmly that you had to respect the man. He could read people like a book and know exactly what they needed to hear. With his tutelage, I've gotten pretty good at this, but still pale by comparison to what he could do. I imagine that he told the company, figuratively speaking, "Get us in a house or kiss me goodbye."

> The following week, we moved into an upstairs, downstairs, three-bedroom house. The lower floor wasn't finished, but we didn't care because we stayed upstairs for the most part.

> *General Patton is one of my main heroes, by the way.* Certainly not his temper, but his knowing what had to be done and making certain that things are done with that objective in mind.
>
> Setting and achieving goals is part of everyone's life. It's a natural part of living, but often times, we don't stick to our plans and it often results in failure. I think the tests of time have taught me to stick to plans.

When I enrolled in the Wyoming, Junior High, at first, it was just like Arkansas and Alabama. It was me alone against the world. I had no physical education classes in either Arkansas, Alabama, or Wyoming, so I didn't really get the masculine bonding of sports like the other kids.

My first friend was named C. I forget his last name, but he looked exactly like W from Alabama whose last name I also forget. (Moving around like we did developed the philosophy of, "*The names change, the faces don't.*")

One day, C and I ate our lunch and then went outside to the back of the school where the track was. We just wanted to talk and have some fun. We were far away from the school, on the far side of the track, when we saw four other boys coming towards us, one of which I had been having a little bit of trouble with anyway.

Our disagreements were nothing much to speak about and in truth, I totally forget what the context was, but by the look in their eyes, they were looking for trouble. **Physical trouble!**

Since they were between us and the school building, I told Clark to get away from me. I told him to circle around and get the principal. He did not want to leave me, but I knew I was in mortal danger and that if he didn't go get help, then there would be none. I repeated my instructions over and over, then waved him off. My guts were trembling. I was nauseous. I knew I could be killed all too easily by fisticuffs. I felt like my heart was going to burst.

> They say in times of great peril that people see their whole life flash before their eyes. Well, I am here to tell you that it is not a myth. I don't know why it happens, just that it does.

3 Lifetimes In 1

> In a fraction of a second I saw and relived my life and hurt all over. It was a deep sadness and a profound sense of failure. I had done nothing even worthy of a footnote. All I had done was handle pain and a large collection of great family experiences.

The four boys were rapidly approaching with angry scowls on their faces. Behind and to the sides of me were five-foot chainlink fences and beyond to the rear was the crest of a hill. There was nowhere to run.

In my younger years, before the burn, I wouldn't have hesitated to take on all four. You see, in addition to being an outgoing, physically-active kid, I also loved to fight and would duke it out with anyone, even up to four. I had a special pair of heavy boots that I would wear on days that I was expecting a fight. Kicking those boots on someone's leg was a great tactic to gain advantage over them.

I fought to win!

RA, in Glen Rose, and I fought weekly almost. We really split winning the fights 50/50. Of course, as an adult, I realize now that no one "*wins*" a fight. Both parties simply show their stupidity. At the time though, it was "*loads of fun*". It's a shame, but I never got to know him personally. Maybe if I had, we would have even liked each other.

> I think I liked to fight more as a sporting event than in anger. Not that I liked boxing or ever have, but as a physical activity, it was fun.

MM, who had failed a grade, and I fought about once a year. He was quite a bit bigger than I was and I always lost, but you know, the winner of a fight is usually whomever has the most friends in the vicinity.

Fighting is pitiful.

Where I really messed up is when I started trying to meet kids alone after school. I was alone, true to my word, but they never were. One time, I was staring six kids in the face in between two buildings and I was just plain scared. It was D.

I never understood D. I guess it was his way in playing, but he would always say it was his S.W.A.T. team. At the time, the TV show, S.W.A.T., was very popular and I guess D liked the show. He may have been one of those special people who got confused between fiction and reality, I don't know.

Regardless, on one of those times when I was too daring for my own good, Michael, who was in high school at the time, came around the corner where I was and just said, "*Let's go, Mark*'" I was so very thankful to see him.

This time, there was no one but me to look out for me. I was all alone. They were coming at me and they were going to beat me to a pulp and probably kill me due to the weakness in my graft tissue.

I was very relieved when I saw the principal, my friend C beside him, come up behind them and waved them off telling them to get back inside the building.

The principal pulled me in his office afterward and wondered why I was back there in the first place. Well, when they were passing out honesty, I bought the farm, truck, house, land, tractor, roosters, and everything else. Growing up, kids always lie at some point, but I never lied much. Mother and Daddy had always told me that honesty was always the best policy and that I would get in far less trouble with them if I simply told the truth. Heck, it seemed like a simple plan to me, so that's exactly what I did with everything in my life.

I told the principal about my graft tissue, where it came from, how thick it was, color, dimples, and all else. I think I even pulled up my shirt and showed him. In fact I know I did, but he immediately told me to put the shirt back down.

I was a bundle of nerves, quivering, and couldn't hardly talk. I was crying on the field outside and now inside his office. I guess he took pity on me as he listened earnestly and afterward just let me wait until my face cleared and then sent me back to my regular class which had already started.

It was shortly after this that I would meet a friend that would totally change my life forevermore. I was riding home on the bus one day and sitting in a seat by myself when this redhaired kid sits down beside me and introduces himself as R.

He was a medium height dude that looked a little strange to me. He had a backpack that he sat in the seat and I think he wore dark framed glasses at that time also that were held to his head with a back spandex strap. I remember he had a lot of freckles too. Well, after we got through the general hubbub that you go through with every new person that you meet, he starts talking about girls and what he liked about them.

At the time, I was too introverted to even think about girls, but this dude asks me what kind of ass I liked. Did I like tight asses or big? I have to admit, at the time, this guy was kind of scaring me at this point

> **The truth is, he was pulling me out of a deep shell that I had built around myself.**

Do you know how a caterpillar cocoons itself as a protection while it changes? Well, that was sort of me. I had to come out of my shell at some time or other, but I think it led eventually to a point of no return for me. I will tell you more about that later.

7

Unravel the mind

It turned out that R and I lived in the same trailer park. In the 3 months or so left in junior high, we got to be good friends. Dare I say GREAT… And as you might suspect, as often times happened with best friends, we had no classes together so we made time to be together in addition to on the bus. The fact that we lived about 25 yards from each other helped a lot.

Life was finally looking up for me and as I remember back, living in Wyoming was the absolute best that I had ever been in my youth. With R in my life, things had finally started to settle down for me, both in my mind and my activities.

During the summer, R and I designed our own version of a rocket. It was the darndest thing you ever saw with two top and two bottom curved fins (on opposing sides) and four fragments of pencils that were glued to the outside edges. R wanted to design it that way to look sort of like a plane. I cautioned him that it would not be enough to stability to fly straight, but he told me no that every rocket in the world had three to four fins and wanted something different.

I talked and talked and talked until I was blue in the face and then finally gave up. So, when we tried to test fly our rocket in the large field behind the trailer park, it went up all right and then we had to run for our lives.

R simply ducked while I hit the dirt because the rocket was going everywhere. Mom and Dad who supervised our test flight were playing the duck and dodge game too.

Have you heard the story about how NASA's start was? In the early goings, it was a disaster. Failure after failure... Rockets would lay down on their side at launch time and simply explode. Others would launch in the air about 20 feet and then and either take a nosedive and explode when they hit the ground or simply explode in midair. It was not until NASA hired some German engineers did the program get on its feet.

These German engineers, incidentally, came over from Nazi Germany and NASA didn't want *American rockets* to be associated with anything connected with the Nazis. They made the engineers change their names to not be associated with the American technology which was really German. After our fiasco of a launch, I was reminded of those engineers long ago. Not that I would ever changed my name or anything, but I felt that we failed. Mom said that at least we tried and that was more than a lot of people could say.

I guess she was right.

We went on a hike to some mountains behind where we lived along with R's older brother. R said it was easy to get to and Mom let us all go together. She had had time to get to know R as well as his brother and knew that both were good guys. So, we set out fairly early one morning after searching for a lost watch of mine. I was actually almost frantic about finding my watch. Ever since our car wreck and even before, details bothered me. I was very picky about most things in my life.

> They call that kind of person a ***perfectionist*** and let me tell you that if you are a ***perfectionist***, that's an easy way to drive yourself crazy. Over the years, I have learned to be much more relaxed. People around me would not say so, even my Mom, but I am far easier going that I used to be and it has made life much less stressful. There are lots of issues that I still do fret with, but by and large, I do not worry about a lot of things that I used to almost obsess over.

Back to my story...

It turns out, that after hiking about 45 minutes, I found out that R left out one critical detail and I was not too happy with the omission. As it turns out, in order to get where we were going, we had to cross a cable bridge over the Green River.

For those of you don't know what a cable bridge is, let me explain. You have steel pillars at both ends of the river and, in our case, there was a steel pillar in the center of the river, all anchored into the ground, or the river, with concrete. We all are familiar with the Golden gate Bridge in San Francisco, California. That is a suspension bridge which is exactly like the cable bridge except the former does not support a highway.

While I'm at it, let me explain something to the people down south. Green River, Wyoming had two seasons: winter and July. Therefore the water in the river never rose above 50° and that's in the middle of July. I remember a professional swimmer, for a charity event and fundraiser for The March of Dimes or something like that, got into an insulated rubber suit and was going to swim 3 miles downriver and asked that people pledged money per mile that he made.

Well, he completed over 2 miles, but nearly died of hypothermia. So, now you understand where we were at as well as the circumstances.

R climbed up on the first tower and started across. Agreed, these were 1 inch cables capable of withstanding a heck of a lot, but when he got halfway between the first and second pillar, *this crazy fool* who was my **best friend** that drew me at least partway out of my cocoon, began swinging on the thick cables like a deranged monkey begging for bananas at the zoo.

This terrified me. I'm sure he had done this dozens of times before, but I knew that one mistake could be almost certain death at the hands of an icy and swift river. I had the advantage or disadvantage depending on your point of view, of coming from an entirely different background than he was used to.

He kept coaxing me to swing with him and have fun with the adventure of it all. I swung a little bit, but not much, knowing all too well the consequences of slip ups.

We got across fine and went on to the peak. Looking over the edge, it looked like about a 60-foot drop. I looked over the edge two or three times, but having a fear of heights proved to be a damper on my fun.

We ate the sandwiches that we had brought and talked quite a bit about life, school, past, present, and future. R was always someone I could always talk and relate to. There were other friends that I had in my life, but none like R.

Sometimes we have "*special*" friends in our lives that obscure the boundaries of what is normal. We have a special rapport with them and it remains so forever. What causes this bond is in the history between the people like the mystery of why two people fall in love over the course of time. The flow of time has many eddies and currents that it flows in and they repeat throughout history it seems like.

The same currents have a tendency to sweep two people together in the same direction. Ah, the ties that bind us together as a group are a miraculous thing. I lost track of R for almost 20 years, but the eddies of time brought us back together through the miracle of social media networks. As much as we may cuss and sometimes despise them for the instantaneous relaying of our thoughts and ideas, they do serve a useful purpose. That is, if we use them correctly and not to the detriment of others.

Once the summer was over, of course we went back to school. A*s Murphy's Law* will have it every time, R and I had but one class together. I began playing my trumpet in the high school band under Mr. L. He was a warm, friendly sort and a proactive, detail minded person. I really enjoyed working with him.

Anyway, our band marched in competitions, played in concerts, competed, and won many awards. We did quite well and I loved the music.

I didn't care for marching. All of those steps to learn were tiring on the body and the mind, but I really liked playing in the stands during the games. <u>Basketball season was a bit different.</u> We just had to sit up in the bleachers and play all of this upbeat and modern music instead of those march tunes: **the fun stuff**. Concert season came at the end of the year and that was fun too. Mostly it was showpieces and emotional, thought provoking music, which I found to be easy on the mind.

In the band, I made another friend by the name of J. He was two grades above me and already had a learner's permit for driving. His hair was curly and he had green eyes, but his most recognizable features were his green teeth. They weren't all green mind you, just the parts next to the gums. It looked gross.

That didn't dissuade me because Mother and Daddy always taught me to treat everybody the same way that they treated me. I really think his teeth were more a matter of a health condition that he had rather than bad hygiene. I'd like to think so anyway.

3 Lifetimes In 1

J and I spent many nights over at his house listening to music and talking. Although I had other friends like C, E, and others, it was mainly J and R that were my friends. They were friends with one another too and that made things a lot smoother as far as getting together as a group.

J is actually where my interest in computers started. He had a RadioShack TRS-80 computer (years later they were called Trash-80's, but this was after the Commodore's came out) with all of 16 K. Ha! Remember those things? Yes, if you are of the younger crowd, you probably weren't even born by the time those things went the way of the dodo bird, but at that time, these things were hot stuff. They were the first real home computers and the first ever released to the general population. I liked them.

J would show me the things that he programmed and I would learn the techniques of how to write them. I used pen and paper, to write a few programs myself, but they were nowhere near as advanced as his.

I found it awesome that he had taken a tank combat board game and converted it to a program.

He and I went to the mall together often. While books were our favorite thing to look at, we shopped for electronics and, as typical high school kids do, ate a lot.

I really looked up to J as a friend and mentor.

C and I were fond friends also and I even went on vacation with him and his parents. He was the only child left at home and wanted me to go with them for company I suppose so we cleared it with parents and then off we went North to Yellowstone Park for a three day excursion.

It was loads of fun, but the most thrilling part was on the way back. We stopped in a town on the way back and rode a raft, along with some other people, over the Red River rapids. We traveled a couple of miles downriver with waves crashing into our sides. We were not strapped in and only had cords of rope to hang on to.

As the waves repeatedly pounded into us, our clothes became drenched with river water and our bodies waterlogged. As the raft bobbed up and down, my hands gripped ever tighter around the half-inch nylon cords. Even with as much fun as I was having with C smiling, laughing at my side, I couldn't help but look at the blue-white water gushing below the side of the raft and wonder what would happen if I suddenly turned loose of everything.

Surely they had a plan in place for such an event... Things had not been so great in my life at that point. Mom and Dad had been super and we regularly went on trips. There were some great times to be sure, but something was missing in my life: me.

Well, I decided not to do what I was thinking, but that thought was only a start.

You see, suffering from physical pain is the easy part. I had three months of recovering from the wreck. I was a tough cookie with a high tolerance to pain. I could handle the physical stuff, but the mental trauma would last the rest of my life and I didn't know it.

3 Lifetimes In 1

Seeing and dealing with the aftereffects, that is tougher than I can ever say. I had no idea that my emotional weaknesses were not normal. *It's crazy.* Some things about that time haunt me to this very day. It's not humanly possible for me to ever forget the things that were imprinted in me with such extreme force.

There were good times too, like National History Day in which R helped me construct an exact copy of the Alamo, complete with written report. I got an "*Excellent*," at the local level and a rating of "*Good*," at state.

> **I will always remember Dad and I's cave exploring adventures. We saw some really awesome sites in those caves.**

Mom, Dad, and I's went on uncounted scenic and fun trips like Ouray, Colorado and Wasatch National Forest. Ouray is close to Silverton. It's a great place to fish, pan for gold, tour actual mines, and all kinds of fun stuff.

Wasatch... Now there was a place to fish, hunt, sightsee, camp, and *be happy*. We made numerous trips up there. On one hunting trip for deer, Dad and I built an 8' x 8' camp fire and it was so cold that 6-inches from the fire, you couldn't feel any heat.

I started the night inside the tent, but quickly moved outside by the fire. When I did, Dad laid inside the tent. Come morning, Dad's hair was layered with ice and I discovered that I had scooted so close to the fire, that the plastic outside layer of my snow boot had melted. We were "*making memories*".

The only problem was that I always had to come back to "**me**".

> I don't wonder why a lot of soldiers come back from combat situations and attempt suicide. Their nerves get friend like an egg by the intensity and unexpectedness of war. It would be like my wife getting zapped with intense electricity several dozen times per day for several years. When the zapping was taken away, she would still respond however she had been trained.
>
> Soldiers have to be trained to do the unthinkable acts that go with the protection of a nation and I have the utmost respect for them. They have the added complication of going from a high pressure situation where they know all the rules to an environment with different pressures or no pressure and where their "*trained actions*" need to conform to society actions. Unfortunately, their brains have been "*trained*" to think differently, the military-combat, life-preservation, guilt-laden, ways.
>
> It is very tough to deal with the memories of what you've done. It's nearly impossible to resolve the *person you are* and the *actions you've done*.

Did you know that our minds form pathways every time we think a thought? Over time, these pathways become more defined, deeper, and slowly they become almost impossible to deviate from. For example, if every time I get angry I become physically violent, if, after say five years if I haven't broke that unhealthy reaction, it would become nearly impossible to break the trend.

Fast forward to my situation. I became trapped by my own psychology.

I have told you that my burns were over 42% of my body. The graft donor sites were on my lower abdomen, right above the groin, fronts, backs, and sides of the legs and they were like second-degree burns so you could literally say that the actual percentage of burns on my body were closer to 65 to 75%.

Although clothing covers up the majority of the areas, they didn't cover "all" and I would see those areas daily. Each time that I got dressed, bathed, took off or changed my clothes for any reason, I would see those scars. When you make a mistake, drop and break a glass for instance, you can forget about it and go on with your life. Those scars reminded me daily of the pain that I went through (*and still do*). In the privacy of wherever I happened to be, I would re-live those painful experiences all over again and the memories burned inside of me.

I would often stare at them for long periods of time remembering the pain and trauma associated with treatment. Not being normal skin, I had to moisturize it daily. *It was always there.* I rarely wore shorts for fear of someone seeing the donor sites on my thighs. When I was alone, I would simply stare at them, wanting to cry, but not being able to somehow. I remembered the whirlpool baths and waking up from surgery with grade 15 out of 10 pain and medications being barely able dull my conscious.

> **It hollowed me. Ate me up from the inside and I couldn't get away from it, ever.**

I was at those teenage years where I was becoming sexually aware *(on an adult level)* and wanted to be with teenage girls of my age. Yet, my mind knew about those cares and wouldn't allow me to even approach intimacy. Girls sometimes would come on to me, but I would tremble and on the verge of a nervous breakdown and have to run away as fast as I could.

Pity. Those years should be some of the best times in your life. For me, they were torment. I began dealing with things that I shouldn't and no human being ever should. There were things that were in my life at that time that I will never talk about again with anybody or for any reason. There are things about that time in my life that bring up such powerful emotions in me that it is even hard to even scratch at the surface here.

To make my sexual blockade worse, a friend of ours kept talking about how he was going to take me down the local whore street and get me laid. I knew he was joking of course, but in twisted mind back then, this added to my self-pressures.

I began to talk to myself in my mind. This is because I became trapped in such a never-ending, vicious circle that I thought that I was the only person who could understand what I was going through. I have no idea how long this went on because those times are very foggy. *Almost like a dream...*

I unwittingly picked the one person who could know everything and have all my answers. God became my confidant, wise man, and everything else. Kids have invisible friends, why is it so crazy for someone a bit older to have one too? Yes, it's who, correct. I was seeking answers to my dilemma, trying to help myself. God was my sounding board. In my frame of mind, it was the perfect choice.

I didn't feel that I could talk to anyone about what I was going through. I was embarrassed that I was having troubles. I felt that I should have been able to deal with everything. Everyone around me seemed to be dealing with life okay. I should've been able to also, right? Talking to God preserved my dignity.

IMPORTANT:

By the way, if you ever see anybody having trouble dealing with life and you think that they are at the point of suicide, don't think you can understand what they're going through. You can talk to them. You can nurture them. What you can't do is understand because I assure you that even though I am as explicit as I know how to be about most things that went on during this time, the truth is far, far darker.

I think that unless you've been through it, or have a complete understanding of their life as a psychiatrist, then there is NO WAY to comprehend what is going on and the self pressures involved. That is why people go through years and years of counseling for these matters. No one understands completely. I don't even understand everything that I was going through.

Some say it was because I was playing Dungeons & Dragons at the time. Others claim a holistic cause, but the truth is that it was all because of a multifaceted issue that is beyond normal comprehension.

To illustrate where I was mentally, lets take a normal activity: **swimming**. *Before the wreck*, I always swam bare chested. *Afterward*, I always wore a T-shirt. <u>That's a prime example</u>. It's doesn't look odd on the surface, but it exemplifies my isolation and shielding.

<u>Finally, there came a point of no return</u>. My grades dropped. I failed algebra. I had been placed in something like 8th or 9th chair in band (I had never been lower than 3rd chair until my freshman year. I was away from my friends in the band also). The school, which I had battles with over the years, was telling me that the following year I would have to take P. E. (Physical education) and that frightened me. I visited with my counselor about some problems that I was

having and the physical education. I got nowhere and not a shred of help.

I researched crisis hotlines as a kid would, I guess, and didn't find any. I probably didn't look in the right areas. After not finding anything, I began reading the Bible incessantly.

> There was a young man named SKM at John Peter Smith Hospital. He had a motorcycle accident, I think, and had developed severe bedsores. He was on a Stryker frame which suspends the body in the air and lets the affected areas heal naturally. He and I talked on a regular basis.
>
> When I was about to leave the hospital, SKM sent me, by way of his wife or Mom I think, a King James version of the Bible and autographed it, complete with date, and told me how much he had enjoyed my company. I don't know what happened to him after I left the hospital, but I certainly hope it was good.

Anyway, I said that to tell you that it was SKM's Bible that I started carting around everywhere. My mind had become so skewed as to contemplating the thought of suicide.

3 Lifetimes In 1

I never wanted to die, only to stop thinking. To make the pressures of life go away...

I don't know how many hours, days, weeks, or whatever that this went on because my memories of those times are somewhat skewed. I do remember that I was interested in reading somewhere in the Bible about suicide. I don't think I ever found it directly addressed. I had thought about going back to the cliff where R and I were and jumping, but that seemed too painful. That was exactly what I trying to escape.

The life that I had been living was somehow being dismantled right before my eyes. Each time I tried to do something about it, the situation got worse. I became powerless to control my mind or my life.

My head ached constantly and my nerves were jittery. When I was by myself, which was a lot of the time because Mom and Daddy both worked, unless I was doing an activity that was recreational (like my Atari video games), my mind would always come back to the extreme pressure of my situation. I could barely think. Each day seemed to become more distanced from reality. Although I would get nervous about not being able to do a lot of things that were seemingly simple, I couldn't cry. I felt tired all over most of the time.

To make matters worse, the root cause eluded me.

I had even put a gun to my head several times, but couldn't pull the trigger. Then, I began the beginning of the end. I would bet my life on simple everyday happenings of life. I couldn't even begin to tell you why or how long these games of chance went on because it was like I was doing things unwittingly, more less as an observer.

Finally, January 10, 1982, it came down to the Dallas Cowboys versus the San Francisco 49'ers NFC championship game. Dallas was ahead in the fourth quarter, but Joe Montana made one of his infamous last-minute fourth-quarter drives and Jerry Rice made a touchdown grab in the final seconds. It was the one that they called, "*The Catch*".

So the next morning, I ate breakfast as a last meal, went into Mom and Dad's bedroom, grabbed a .32 pistol, laid down on the bed, and stopped thinking.

Life Three

Before I start the next section, I would like to explain something.

Although people like my Mother, Daddy, brother, family, friends, and all who knew of my situation with the burn were doing their best to provide me with as normal of a life as humanly possible as well as emotionally being there and a reservoir of knowledge for me to lean on, it is my belief, as well as many others, that my mental isolation was so complete that no one and nothing could have stopped what happened.

What brought my problems to the surface with so much force, I will never know. Why would my freshman year have gone so well? Why did my sophomore year go straight downhill? There are about one million questions like that that I would love to know the answers to. I mean, I thought I had my head together. Yes, there were issues, but even with all the facts that I have put together here, I don't understand how I could do such a thing.

The suicide attempt forever altered my future like the wreck did. My Mother has told me many times that I started out to be exactly like my maternal grandfather. I adored him. He was a brash, sharp, forceful, so-and -so at times, but for me I admired his ' take the bull by the horns' attitude. It is something that I have tried to live my life by.

I have found it to be true that it is far, far better to go out and seek what your heart desires (*whether that be love, a problem, or something else*) rather than wait and miss opportunities.

That attitude would serve me well in the years ahead, but it would take me a long time to find myself and that attitude again. The person that I was in my second life was not me and never will be. In truth, you could say that I was never fully recovered and not even truly there. The whole thing is like a long nightmare. There were some good times, yes, and in fact some great times. Some of the greatest times in my life came during those a few years, but they were also some of the worst too. Unfortunately, I would have to go through some more rough times before my mind could get back on track.

8

Crushing Rejoice

<u>This next part I will have to tell you from the way it was told to me.</u>

My sister-in-law, who was living with us at the time, heard a sound that morning but she didn't think anything of it. Later, when she got out of bed, she saw the note that I had wrote and taped to the door of the bedroom.

Starting to read, she was naturally speechless and burst into the bedroom. She said I was lying on the bed with my eyes open and as she walked in, she said that my eyes followed her. She tried talking to me to no avail. When she came around to my right, she was able to see the injury to my head.

Well, the police, ambulance and everyone were called and I was soon flown by helicopter to Salt Lake City, Utah to Children's Primary Hospital. Dr. S operated to remove bullet fragments from my head and gave my parents no hope of my survival.

At that time, God took my life into His hands once again.

I was kept in a drug-induced coma and, three days later, a hematoma made its presence known on my head. Now, a hematoma, for those of you who don't know, is more than a concussion. It alters the blood flow in the area. It can also alter thinking processes and be hazardous to one's health.

Dr. S operated again to remove the hematoma and again gave no hope of my recovery. Everyone suggested that I must have fallen down after the bullet went in, but the hitch in that logic is, I was lying down, so the hematoma must have occurred at sometime prior.

No one could figure out what happened because, outwardly at least, I had appeared so normal. I think there was some speculation as to foul play and I'm sure in each attempted suicide situation, there is a tendency to try and jump to any conclusion except the obvious. But, in my case, the obvious answer was the correct one except it didn't really tell all of the story you are now reading.

Anyway, some weeks later, they finally decided that I was going to survive, but I was going to be a ***mental vegetable*** for the rest of my life. *Do I sound like a mental vegetable to you?* No, I didn't think so. Doctors don't know everything. **There is the God factor**.

Because of the swelling in the brain after the two surgeries, they inserted an instrument into my head that made me sort of look like Frankenstein to monitor the cranial pressure. It got up almost borderline of the point where they would give up but it never made it quite that far. My EEG, that monitors brain activity, was almost flat: *mental vegetable*. They would occasionally pack me in ice because of my temperature. I mean, the outlook with bleak.

I owe a debt of gratitude to a nurse whom I never even met. There was a young doctor at the hospital that wanted to practice doing a tracheotomy on me because I was supposedly not breathing well on my own. This nurse saw this young doctor in my room and pulled Mom and Daddy over to the side. She told them that the ventilator that I was using had went off the previous night and that I was breathing on my own. She warned Mom and Dad not to let this young doctor do the procedure because it was unnecessary.

    After she stated the perilous consequences of her speaking up, which would be loss of her license, Mom and Dad agreed to preserve her anonymity. They also stopped this young doctor from doing the procedure, which I am thankful for.

    Soon after, it was decided that if I ever did regain consciousness and be a living person, vegetable or not, that the Children's Hospital would not be the place for me to be because everything would be undersized for a person of my age. I was transferred to the University Hospital of Salt Lake City. I never even saw the first hospital. It was not a great loss to me, but it is a part of my history that I never saw.

    I don't know how long it was before I was conscious, but I am told that it was about a month. At first, nobody even knew that I could rationalize anything. For all anyone knew, I was just 120 pounds of flesh and not much more than that. Oh, they would play music, talk to me, and talk amongst themselves, but nobody even knew that I was a rational, thinking person at that time.

    I remember them playing music and watching TV. At the time I didn't even know what was going on or what had happened. I was unable to move, speak, eat, drink, or anything else that we consider life. Oh, the autonomic functions were working, but nothing else.

Perhaps I better explain that. When a person shoots themselves in the head, the gun is usually placed at the Temple. This usually ends up wiping out the optic nerve and renders the person blind. When my shooting happened, the bullet entered behind the right temple all but wiping out the motor control center of the brain.

Without any motor control, I was like I said, 120 pounds of flesh. The only things that were working were the autonomic functions of the body like the heart, circulation, tears, breathing, etc.

I didn't know what had happened but I knew that it must've been very serious. I was as confused as I'm sure they must've been. Every now and then the stodgy old doctor would come in and talk to Mom and Dad. Then, they started pushing me in a wheelchair around the hospital. Again, I was dazed and confused about the whole situation. I had no idea what had happened. My memory back before the incident was mostly about the good things such as my friends, school, and stuff like that. I had no idea what was going on.

Since I had nothing else to do, I started reading the signs in the hallways. I would do anything to keep my mind active: watch TV, listen to music, listen to people, think about computers, etc. Anything...

3 Lifetimes In 1

One day, Mom was leaning over me, Dad was behind her and he held up a little piece of paper with a simple note on it saying, "give Mother the raspberry." Well, for those of you who don't know, a *raspberry* is the act of sticking your tongue out and blowing. So, I did it as he suggested.

You see, my Dad was one sharp cookie. He watched my eyes and saw that I was reading the signs in the hospital. The easiest way that he could test his theory was his note regarding one of the very few things that I still could control.

So what did I do? Of course... I gave my Mother a wet tongued raspberry. You would've thought it was one of John Elway's final few seconds Super Bowl victories. I can certainly understand their reaction. **To them, it was monumental!** The young son that they had grown to love and cherish was, *at least to some degree*, in this nonfunctioning body somewhere. It had been verified that I could read and respond. The true test would come a bit later. Sure, I could read and respond, but was I mentally aware?

I remember my roommate was not near as fortunate as I was. I can't remember his name, but he was a head injury patient too. Oh yeah! D. He moaned quite a bit and was not near as cognitive as I was. I remember his Dad would come in and talk to him for hours. In the recreation room seeing his head jutted forward, sort of like mine was, *saddened me.*

Sometimes we would go down there too. Although the hospital rooms were big, sometimes we were more comfortable, space wise, in the larger room. I remember D's

> Dad physically pulling his son's head back and asking him if that was more comfortable. It always seemed to be a strain for him, but D always moaned, "*Yeah.*"

Was that what was in store for me? Not being able to do anything has many disadvantages, but not being able to communicate was by far the worst. I cried for days on end it seems like. I remembered the life that I had and wanted this nightmare to end.

> I did cry quite a bit. You see, the second worse shock that human being can stand is severe burns. The first is a severe head injury. When a head injury wakes from the drug-induced coma, they are either angry or sad. *It's really another form of Post Traumatic Stress Disorder (PTSD).* For me, it was sadness about everything. (Over the many years, I have found things that help me deal with the PTSD reasonably well.)
>
> There is one thing I'll say about being in a chair for as long as I have and that is it gives me the quality of inconspicuousness. No matter what I say or do *that quality* shines through in most situations. Either people talk freer around me because they ignore my intellect or they realize my situation and talk to me as if they are conversing with their subconscious.
>
> In either case, it gives me a chance to see them from a totally new and different aspect than most. I just hate the type

3 Lifetimes In 1

> that discounts me from having the same adult feelings as they do however, from love to lust to anger and all else.

After a few weeks went by came the day of recognition. Like I said, I had loved music and as a result, they had music playing all the time. Mostly, they were my cassette tapes: Queen, Doobie Brothers, and many more. Mom and Daddy were at the front of my bed and on this day, I was really enjoying the music. The song, "*Come Sail Away*" by Styx began to play.

If you don't remember or don't know that song, it starts off very slow and soft with beautiful words about a new beginning, being responsible for ones self, and setting a new course across an unexplored ocean. It goes on to say the several Angels appeared and sang a song of hope.

I began mouthing the words to the song in time with the music. I didn't realize it at the time, but those just so happened to be the perfect words both for them to realize that I was completely cognitively aware with my memories and thinking ability intact. Those words were a good outline for my future. It was the start of my third lifetime that was graciously given to me by a loving God.

The simple fact that I was alive was a miracle, the fact that I was sane, much less with memories and ability to reason intact was unfathomable by any reasoning that we flawed humans can conceive.

Mom and Dad were just thrilled that I had my memories and was cognitive. If I had known then what I need now, I would've probably reacted differently other than just a smile and probably a blank stupor expression. I was just liking the song. I knew that my mind was okay and didn't realize that it was ever in question. I didn't realize the significance of that moment then, but in reflection, it was ***monumental***.

After that, we worked out blinking signals. One blink for yes, two blinks for no, a long blink for "I love you". They told the doctor about the incident and it was at that time that Dr. S began to talk "*TO*" me instead of "*AT*" me "*OR*" around me. I noticed that he seemed vaguely interested and really unconcerned. It was probably just my impression, but first impressions are tough to get over.

Not long after that, I started therapy, occupational and physical. DB was the head of occupational therapy whom I started to work with. I had a Plexiglas lap tray, which he would put a rubber ball on top of, and then he would put my hand on top of that. The idea was for me roll the ball on the lap tray. *Sounds simple right?*

It's not so simple when you have no motor skills at all. It was really tough at first and he would use a vibrator on the muscles to try and get them to do their job. Simple stuff like that is about all that we would start out with.

Physical therapy, which is gross motor control, was a bit different. ME was my therapist and he would try to get me to bend and straighten my arms and legs. *He was a pretty nice guy*. In fact, they were both nice. DB was more businesslike than ME, but they were both good.

After I got better situated physically, they started me on eating and drinking food. That may seem simple also, but I literally had to relearn how to do it. I couldn't feed myself because my arms didn't work, my Mom and Dad were always there to help me.

At first, the food items were puréed. *Have you ever tasted that stuff???* It is kind of bad and, in fact, Mother later told me that she thought that it was horrible. *I found it edible but just barely*. I would get choked easily on both food and drink.

Folks, I didn't even know how to swallow food or even any liquid. That's how much like an infant I was. I remembered doing both, but couldn't quite do either on my own without nearly killing myself from choking. Can you really understand how mentally painful that was?

It's very aggravating when you can't even do the simplest of tasks on your own. A high level of frustration set in very quickly with both therapy and daily living tasks the likes of which I never experienced before. I still deal with it even today in various degrees.

> Please forgive me if this sounds too much of a step-by-step process, but I want you to totally understand the point that I was totally starting over from scratch (with family help, of course). *I mean, I couldn't do anything.* Things that we take for granted, even as infants, seemed monumental achievements to me. Slowly, I got to where I could both eat and drink without much difficulty.

My brother brought me new cassettes every once in a

while which I much appreciated. It was a break from the monotony of wake-up, take pills, go to therapy, be with family, and basically try to keep my mind active. Though everyone tried to keep my mind alert by doing various things, there were a lot of times when I had to try and keep myself going.

> I can't imagine what it was like for them, Mom, Dad, Michael and all the rest. *It must have been hell for them.* It wasn't like after the wreck where I could at least talk to them. They were trying to relate to a person that they loved who wasn't unconscious and couldn't even speak to them. To make matters worse, we lived in Green River, Wyoming and I was in Salt Lake City, Utah. It was not like we could see each other every day because those two places are about a three-hour drive apart.

When Mother and Daddy told me what was happening, and I'm told that they did on numerous occasions, I didn't remember from one time to the next so each time, it had the same shock effect, *I cried my eyes out every time.* I can't describe what it's like to wake up in a nightmare (*after the wreck, after the shooting*) to find oneself in a whole new world. Each time was a totally different place with new rules and nearly everything was changed. The only thing constant was family.

The place that I was in was a totally different place from anything that I had known, or even dreamed about, or even thought was possible. The world that I was in was totally reprehensible and despicable. The fact that this time was of my own making was totally unbelievable to me and vile. It made me feel like a lowdown, creepy, scumbag.

> I can only describe about three months, I think, before the shooting as me walking around as a prisoner in my own body looking out. No control. Seeing what was happening, but unable to alter anything. Like I said before, hindsight is 20/20, or at least I assume that. I say, "*I think*", because I'm not even sure of my own mind during that time. I can only tell you of the events that I saw, not the "*why's*" for everything. I know only the facts and what I think that I was thinking and feeling. I'm not certain of anything during that time.

Each time I heard what had happened I cried and cried and then cried more. I felt that I had been violated in the worst possible way. It is even hard to fathom now after all the years the how and why of what happened. I know what happened only because I lived it. Somehow, God took pity on this soul. Why? *I couldn't even begin to guess.* All I know is that I'm here because of His mercy on a soul that was trapped by past events.

I wrestled with the facts of the tragedy endlessly. My remorse had no end, but over the years I have discovered that, *in my opinion*, me and everyone else were powerless to do anything to help prevent this heinous tragedy.

> Endless tears came. The Greeks could not have written the facts of my life unto this point. Simply put, the news that my condition was by my own hand crushed me. At that point in my life, I didn't know who I was. Who was this Mark Wayne Allen who could do such a thing? Everything that I thought that I knew about myself was rendered moot. I had lost myself in this menagerie of tumultuous feelings about how my body could physically do this vile thing.

Those days seem more like a nightmare after the

nightmare. I have had a dream within a dream. Well, my life before the wreck seemed like my real life. I knew that those days were over and there was nothing to do but march forward. I had to try to do that once again. <u>I had to try to pick up the pieces</u>. The wreck broke my life up into a million parts, but the shooting shattered me into uncountable pieces.

When I started whispering, it was in a coherent manner. I started whispering in full sentences, sort of like I am writing here. I remember being in occupational therapy one day and laying on a mat. DB was absent that day and so JD was lying behind me trying to get my spasms, which had been very violent recently, to ease off. In walks this guy, whom I didn't know at the time, and he leans over and starts talking to me.

This guy was astonished that I was even talking and even said that he didn't know how I was able to do that. Much later, I learned that that man was Dr. S who had evidently discovered that I was whispering coherently, and had to come see for himself because he thought that there was no possible way. *People often forget the God factor!*

After that moment, my memories of those three months at the University of Salt Lake City hospital are kind of blur, but I do remember having speech therapy with a lady that I thought was an incredible bore.

The one memory that stands out in my mind of her is that she asked me one of the dumbest questions that I ever heard of. She asked me if I ran out of gas, what would I do. I told her that I would switch to the other tank (*in those days there were no such things as double-tanks. If you had extra gas, then you had a switch to go between two tanks.*)

Well, she didn't like that answer and asked me which vehicle we normally drove. I told her the truck so she asked me the same dumb question again referring to our family vehicle. I said switch to the other tank. Her face turned even redder and she said, "Okay, Mark, you are in an ordinary vehicle with just one tank…" I swear, the absurdity of some people.

Not long after that, I was asked what I thought about her. When I gave my astute opinion that she was a boring moron, they switched me to the older speech therapists who comically related to me. *He was the only man that I ever knew who could roll his tongue and then whistle through it.*

Mom rolled me down to the gift shop where I could look at all the neat stuff every now and then. Well, I saw a red booklet with a picture of a cartoon cat and told her that I would like to have it. Well, she thought it was overpriced and, I don't think really realize what it was. She didn't buy it. Michael rolled me down to the gift shop a few days later and asked me to pick out anything that I wanted. Ha Ha

There it was, my chance. I told him that I wanted that booklet. It just so happened to be Garfield's first book and we read that sucker day in and day out with big belly laughs on each page. The whole family enjoyed that book to the extreme. That was one of the better diversions that I had in that three-month period. I think we actually got Garfield's second book while I was in there also.

Mark Wayne Allen

> **If my playing one against the other sounds mischievous, you're probably right. At the time though, it was my only means of controlling my surroundings.**

> Everyone who is at a total loss to do much of anything learns to manipulate people very quickly. From this, they also grow extremely adept at quickly assessing situations and since the price is high for them if anything is even a half-inch out of place, they seem like perfectionists.
>
> My wife can tell you that I get obsessive and launch a mad hunt if I loose track of anything, no matter how small. The cost for me to have an item I may need to be at an unknown place is huge since I can't hunt it at my leisure.

Mother and Daddy just so happened to ask me about Dr. S one day and wanted my opinion of him. *It was a natural thing to do.* Sure, I told them that he was an old stick-in-the-mud who didn't care about anyone or anything and that I didn't think he cared whether I lived or died. As I look back on it now, that was a bold statement, especially about one's doctor.

Well, I didn't know this at the time but they told Dr. S and I mean he totally changed his approach to me. I have never seen such a change in a person so quickly. From then on, he was all smiles and popped a few wisecracks when he came to see me. His cold, almost lifeless, green eyes from before twinkled now as he talked.

3 Lifetimes In 1

To a guy that spent his days talking with parents and family and the drudgery of therapy, this was a welcome relief kind of inspired me to tell you the truth. From the actions of Dr. S, I learned that there was more to life than just trying to live and recover.

This is not to say that Mom, Dad, family, and friends were not there for me in all respects (even with fun and games), but it's like when a kid starts pre-K or even kindergarten. All that they know before then is family, friends, and maybe a neighbor or two, whether they are young or old. Most kids are nervous that first day. They soon meet new people and are exposed to many different things that they never even knew existed before. That kind of experience sort of rejuvenates the mind. It catapults you away from a small, isolated, insulated arena to a new and different world with all kinds of new attitudes, beliefs, and concepts.

Yes, there were doctors and nurses all around me giving me alternative different experiences, but Dr. S's approach was new and refreshing. *That's the difference maker!*

Things were going well with occupational therapy and DB but not so much in physical therapy. You see, in addition to being curious about everything and thus easily distracted, ME and I were going around and around both from my lack of attention to therapy and my mental outlook.

You see, an open head injury (*with internal damage*) like mine doesn't really "*clear*" until about one year after the incident. Until then, there is the emotional volatility that I mentioned earlier, cloudy thinking, and to some degree value judgments are more difficult. Well, I really had a problem with the whole incident happening at my hand. *I did it.* That is something that I've had to live with ever since it happened.

> Living with that is no easy thing. Even knowing the facts of my case backwards and forwards, plus the mitigating factors, it still doesn't make living with the situation any easier. For years when I was asked about what put me in a wheelchair, because of the religious and societal stigma to suicide, I would say that it was caused by a wreck.
>
> Being an honest person, I quivered down deep in my soul each time I evaded the issue. I don't know how many years that I did that. Imagine if you had chosen to be a drug lord after high school and you had come from a Christian family. Now, suppose that you are like I was, an extremely honest person.

I want to tell you a humorous story before I continue. As a kid, I think I was four-years-old, I had a habit of pouncing in mud holes. Mom had warned me not to jump in mud holes anymore. Fast forward to a day later. Michael was walking with a friend and I was tagging along behind them. When I came in the house, Mom asked me why my pants were wet.

I told her that Michael and his friend had jumped over a mudhole and that I jumped too, but my little legs weren't long enough and I didn't make it all the way across.

Now that's honesty!

Anyway, I was gone for a while but now I'm back to finish my story. As you can see, I was the epitome of honesty.

The job of the drug lord *(above)* or maybe a hit man are some of the worst examples that I can think of and it still comes short of what I've had to deal with. My chair is obvious and the most common question is what happened to put me in it.

After many years, I wearied of the nagging feeling of not telling the complete truth although my answer was correct in a manner of speaking. I decided that I'd much rather have the truth be known. The consequences of dealing with the emotional turmoil, skirting around the truth, was too much in conflict with my honest nature. Of course, over the years, I have learned how to sum up in just a few words the long and detailed story.

Like I was saying, in physical therapy ME couldn't really get me to cooperate and put effort into the exercises. First, there were the distractions, but he started taking us in a room by ourselves and he started talking to me like a person and trying to find out what the problem was.

I was *(and am)* hardheaded. I know that. I didn't realize the importance of therapy. In fact, I didn't realize a lot of things back then that I wish I did. At the time, I was way too centered on what happened and didn't want to let it happen again. Long story short, I didn't want to do any therapy because I was not going to let a repeat performance of the shooting happen.

We fought like cats and dogs. Him trying to do therapy… me, resisting and uncooperative… It was a case of the proverbial unstoppable force meeting the immovable object. *Who would win?* Well, I discovered much later that there was no way for me to win except to comply, which I didn't do.

I would cry. Eventually, he would too. But, along the way, we became friends or more like adversaries who appreciated the other side. No, we were friends, but we could've been better friends had I not been so hardheaded.

In addition to speech therapy, physical therapy, occupational therapy, I also started seeing RM. He was a psychologist. He and I would talk for quite a while at a time. I don't remember much about him, but I know from Mom that it was his assessment that the shooting incident was related to posttraumatic stress disorder from the wreck, which is a judgment that has been upheld by everyone since.

> **I do remember that we would occasionally play chess together. I guess he was checking my cognitive abilities.**

Dr. S, in his changed mannerism, one day came to my room and offered me a chance to get out of the hospital for a while. He pulled out a coin from his pocket, flipped it, and asked me to guess heads or tails. I said heads and he lifted his hand slightly and asked me if I wanted to guess again.

Well, I thought about that for a moment. In the hospital, I had known security basically all of my life. I was worse than an infant when I woke up from that coma and really wasn't much better off right then. I felt my stomach and my guts quivering at the thought of leaving the security that I had known, but I said tails anyway.

Of course, it was tails and so that next morning we loaded me into some vehicle, I can't remember which, and went to the zoo. We had a good time despite my reservations and it was a good step to resolve the dependency that I had built up in being hospitalized.

Not a great many people have been through the kind of institutionalization that I have and so I can only hope that you would understand. To me, waking up from the coma, I had to take on an entirely new life and one that I never had any conception of. Neither did anybody else in the family. It was a new experience with new rules for each one of us.

Mark Wayne Allen

9

Realistic Determination

I was really nervous when I was released from the hospital. On the ride home, I cried my eyes out uncontrollably. We had moved around all over the country and I had seen friends come and go. This was no exception save one thing. I had been reborn again in the hospital and was starting from ground zero.

If you think you know what Ground Zero is, I beg to differ. Most people think of it as losing everything that you own and all your friends. Most family is always going to be there for better or worse unless you are an only child with no relatives and your parents died off a while back or you are from a dysfunctional family. Other than those exceptions, that's Ground Zero for most people. No assets except for the clothes on your back...

Let me tell you what Ground Zero actually is. It is the loss of all of your bodily control, barely even able to speak or move, and to be **totally dependent** on other people. Not only was I losing the people that I had met and were friends with, but I couldn't even pee without a catheter to keep me from wetting myself. **No hands. No arms. No legs. No feet.** *No control of anything* and I was going away from the only security that I had known in my three-month life. I was fortunate that I had speech.

Mom and Dad were both there, but there was some insecurity there. Granted, they had done everything, learned everything, had talked to me about everything, but that's quite different than being totally reliant on them as a totally dependent teenager. <u>I was less than an infant</u>. My only asset was my mind. Even when I was living at home before, I was not relying on them to this degree, ever.

And so I cried thinking about the people, friends, and security that I was leaving behind. Psychologists might call it separation anxiety. And mind you, it was not only the people, but the building and the routine as well. *The structure.* In my frail mind this was enough to lock my unclear mind and have me fixated on the things of the past.

I understood that we were going to a new home as well, not the one I left behind. You see, after the shooting, Dad could not stand to be in the house where the shooting happened (*understandable*), so in one weekend, he and some of our friends had moved us lock stock and barrel to another house.

Let me explain something about the houses in Wyoming. Ninety-percent of them were two stories. The idea was that the heat from the lower level would rise to the upper and keep the house warmer. Most of them, including ours both past and present, had a front door that opened halfway between the upper and lower levels.

Let me also explain that I was in a reclined wheelchair, with my head on a pillow that was resting on top of an extension of the back.

Well, Mom and Dad backed me up to the staircase going towards the upper level and Dad began to pull, with Mom pushing from the bottom. To me, this was nerve-racking. We were about halfway up when we inadvertently discovered that the headpiece extension where the pillow was laying and my head was resting, was not affixed to the chair and slid out.

Down the stairs we went, all three of us. It was a miracle that my chair didn't bowl over Mom and that Daddy, who carried my head in his hands all the way back down, didn't topple over face first and wind up in the hospital himself. But, no, God was taking care of us that day, all three of us. He somehow took care of us well-meaning simpletons.

> **After the excitement, we went up the stairs again with Dad grabbing the handles of the chair this time.**

They showed me around the house for what seemed like a long time. I appreciate the kindness and delicacy that everyone showed because at the time, I was just trying to get even a small feeling of stability and security. Given what had happened I don't think anyone could be totally at peace with the situation.

At the time, I couldn't even hold my head up from a pillow very long. *I was totally dependent.* My guts ached with pure emotional and physical turmoil. They knew that I was trying to come to grips with my present reality. Balancing my past with the present was proving to be difficult, but my parents, and everyone else were doing their best.

In hindsight, they probably didn't take enough time for themselves. Of course, I could be wrong. We were all dealing with an extremely emotional situation. I was just trying to survive and they were to.

By day, my Dad worked at building the soda ash plant for Brown & Root, which meant it was Mom and I all day. Bless her heart, she was extremely kind, generous, and whatever else good one could ever say. She would do her own brand of occupational therapy and emotional therapy, like letting the dog in for a while. Snuffy knew, and animals usually do, that something was wrong or different, but he didn't care. He loved me just the same, sort of like Mom and Dad.

We would all talk about the present and the future just trying to adapt ourselves to the situation that we were faced with. No one dwelled upon the past, which was probably a good thing. It seems like there were a lot of those talks so I guess you could say it was emotional therapy for everybody.

Things happened during the night when I needed someone to assist me: body parts get to hurting, catheter leaks, etc. Well, one night in the very early goings, like the first week, I woke up needing something. Mom was the one that got up and she never was one to get up in a decent mood. Anyway, she got up, which I commend her for. I mean, it was out of love that she even got up, but she was rather foul.

We got through the episode okay and she went on back to bed while I did the same. The next day, she apologized profusely which I naturally accepted but that episode is a good example of how we were all trying to deal with the situation. We were doing the best we could.

> I'm sure with all new situations comes a period of adjustment. I didn't really consider this at the time. When you are living life, you really don't think about the long-term implications of everything that you do or experience. Every now and then someone will realize that, "Hey, this is because of that situation," but that doesn't happen a lot.
>
> Now, the college courses that I've had, have educated me a lot about human psychology. It helps me avoid some of the pitfalls that we all face, but only mildly. I still hold to the same trends of humankind that we all experience. Yes, these natural flaws give us fits, but we all find shortcuts in our minds to the easy answers that fit nearly every situation. These pathways that we build up in our minds get deeper over time and when we encounter the same or similar situations again, our shortcut minds leap to conclusions even without knowing all the facts.
>
> Sorry, a little more of a psychology lesson there.

Anyway, she had said her apologies and I just told her to forget it. There was no use in looking back at that time. Inside, I think I knew that we were all dealing with a lot and as a friend of mine once said, 'There's no use looking back, always keep your eyes in front.'

Over the years, I have found that to be a good advice. One must say that writing this book is a way of looking back. I'm not looking back to evaluate or to try to change anything although I have learned a few things. In fact, I have learned a lot.

Not trying to change the past, or even be concerned by it, was always my Dad's philosophy too. We make mistakes, as I did, we evaluate those through time, and let our future decisions be tempered by the wisdom we've learned. I have looked back on that day in 1982 SO MANY TIMES but I can tell you that it does no good to reconsider those actions.

I can't change what happened. I can't really do ANYTHING about it and I can't change ANYTHING about the day of the wreck. Those things are set in stone now and forever. The past is the past and everyone might as well accept it.

Naturally, I sank into a deep depression very quickly. My friends, R and J, came to visit me a couple of times as well as others, but I don't think I ever saw C again. It was really good to see my old school chums again, but during the day they were busy. They would sometimes come and visit me at the end of the day, but the visits became less frequent as time went on. They had their own world that I was not part of anymore.

It's understandable. Honestly, it is. It boiled down to me, Mother, and Daddy, just like it always had been. I was 16 years old, but while I was in the coma I did have a birthday. *My sweet 16... Yeah, right...* Maybe for most people it was sweet, but my teenage years had started with a bang: *the wreck*. It had continued this way, getting worse until this point and would not get much better for a long time.

> **We were scheduled to move back to Merryville, LA in a few weeks, a move that was born out of necessity as Dad's job was fixing to end in Wyoming.**

One day shortly before our move I called Mom and asked her to let Snuffy in so that I could see him. She had to tell me that Snuffy had dug under the fence because there was a lady dog in heat in the neighborhood. I felt like that dog was a bright spot in my world. He was my only dog after the burn and thus tied to the life that I had once led. I cried my eyes out once again.

In those days, it didn't take much to upset me. Look at me the wrong way, speak a tiny bit the wrong way, breathe the wrong way, loud noises, soft noises, good things, bad things, or any other life events, and I would start boo-hooing.

I couldn't help it. It's like my nerves had been in a frying pan, or better yet, short-circuited. It was terrible! I didn't know which way was up sometimes and I was concerned about everything and nothing. Mountains out of molehills…

Anyway, Mom and Dad did everything they could to find the dog before we left. Of that, I'm sure. But in the end, it wasn't enough and right or wrong, in my crazy world, I had lost a ton of myself once again.

Snuffy, you see, with the first dog that we had ever

had that was, undeniably, my dog. Other dogs that were at our house had always attached themselves to other people in the family. Rigor was Michael's dog. Butch was the whole family's dog. Brutus was Michael's dog. And so on... I had went to the pound in Montgomery, Alabama with Mom and actually picked out Snuffy myself. Getting Snuffy was a huge event in my life because he was *"my"* cherished dog: *"My Pal."*

He was only about a month or two old when we got him and we quickly became friends. He loved cheese and was the first fish dog that I've ever seen. Catch a fish, throw it up on the bank, and that crazy dog would dig a hole and put that fish in. If the fish should flop out of the hole, no worries, Snuffy would put it back in. Crazy, Man, crazy!

R talked about coming to visit us after we got settled somewhere. Dad picked up on the conversation and said he would fly R down after we got settled. I made him promise, which was probably unfair to him, but Dad promised nevertheless. Of course, by the time we got really settled somewhere, R was probably in the middle of his senior year, and as a result, it never happened.

But, like I said, it was an unfair promise made by a father who wanted to reassure a son who was having extreme difficulties both emotionally and physically. For a while, I was going to hold him to that promise, but I later understood how and why he made it. Sometimes extreme circumstances make us do things that are not sensible. Love will too...

So we moved to Merryville by way of a long road trip

3 Lifetimes In 1

with me. At the beginning of the day, I would be laid down on the sofa at the rear of the van because there was no way that I was physically able to ride in my chair that length of time. Not only because I did not have the stamina, but because the roof of the van was not an extended roof and I had to lean my head over very far just to go anywhere.

Of course, Daddy insisted on going through Dumas, Texas even though I warned him that that was a bad town for us. Of course we got stuck again. Not because of snow and ice, but because when we were ready to take off the next morning, the U-Haul truck broke down. *It was a curse! I swear it was a curse!*

After two days of trying to fix the truck, U-Haul sent us another truck to use.

We were getting so hot after coming down from Wyoming to the heat of Texas. You don't really realize how much you acclimate to weather, but just like it took us six months to get used to the thin air up there (Green River, Wyoming was over 6,000 feet up in the Rocky Mountains) and the same six months to acclimate when you come down. (Merryville is about 80 feet above sea level) It was a big change.

What we didn't count on was getting used to the heat again. We were all burning up. To make matters worse, the van was black and the inside of it was like an oven. The van also had no rear air, so in Dumas, Texas, Dad bought and installed a fan in the rear to blow on me. I was okay with the heat, it feels good to me because I like warmer weather anyway, but everybody else was suffering terribly. As long as I had some air stirring around me, I was okay. That fan really did help stir the air.

> **Well, finally we were on the road again and we soon arrived in Merryville, where my Granny was waiting to greet us.**

I was as nervous as a high-priced New York hooker in an Alabama Southern Gospel folk church. I knew that they were family, but I had no idea about how I would be received after doing what I did. *Would they ask me about it?* There was a whole bunch of things that they could have done or asked. I was very afraid of them or confronting anything else that I had known.

I had not had the time to cope, deal, think, or anything else about the incident. Shame had me tightly within its grasp. I think the moment that we pulled up at her house I would've done or said anything not to have to go inside and look at the faces of those family members, Granny, uncles, aunts, and others who I had not had dealings with since the demise.

But, I couldn't run away and I couldn't hide. None of those things were an option for me because I was at the mercy of others and their physical abilities. So, up the steps we went. Every nerve in my body was increasingly on edge. Each step, each inch, family members grew ever nearer and, to my mind back then, it was a horrific situation.

An old man by the name of Mr. TC later made a ramp

for the back door. It was an unsightly thing that was very steep and if it were made available to me today, I would not go up it because I would consider it dangerous. At that time though, it was a good thing to have.

Anyway, when we were at the top of the steps, Dad wheeled me into the den. He turned me around then started me towards the dining room where my Granny was. Dad parked me underneath at the dining table and straight across the table was Granny. She rose up, came around the table, and gave me a big hug and a kiss.

I can't honestly tell you what I was feeling at that moment. I wanted to explain something that I didn't even know how to put into words myself. So, I just sat there. I couldn't do much else at that point. I was crying on the inside.

We made small talk and from there things quickly got sort of normal. I got over my fear of people and one by one they came in to visit and get reacquainted. We made the living room into my bedroom, but to come and go required a lot of finagling and, as I was in a manual chair, somebody had to push me around.

I'm really surprised at how well we adapted and how quickly. Soon, we went into the next town and got in with a psychologist. We visited him, or I did, four or five times before Mom and Dad decided that he was wrong for our needs. I was just getting really comfortable at Granny's doing therapy with Dad everyday and getting used to the people around me and Dad called up DB in Salt Lake City. I forget how long that they talked, but I remember Dad saying that I was making progress. After they hung up, I heard him talk things over with Mom and telling her that if I was making progress that I should be in a rehab somewhere.

    The next thing I knew, and it seemed very quickly, we were going to down to the rehabilitation center in Houston. Well, I got evaluated by all kinds of departments and soon was admitted. Everything was going well, I thought. I was working with D in physical therapy and some red haired lady named MS in occupational therapy.
    For a while they had me going over to another building where this guy would ask me all kinds of different questions. I didn't mind the questions because they were more like brainteasers, which I had always liked. It got my mind active with puzzles at least. Active without trying to deal with this body of mine that didn't work. It was a welcome relief from my somewhat plain daily living.
    Mom and Dad were with me in the hospital a lot of time making sure everything went right. If you don't know what that's like and I'm sure at least 90% of you who are reading this don't, having someone there to look out for your best interest is one of the greatest things there is on this earth. I had parents that loved me and cared about me and would do anything because of this love. They were with me most of the time, but especially in the evenings.

3 Lifetimes In 1

> **Their being there and helping in that position means more than I can ever say.**

> Anyway, I go and visit this guy for a couple of weeks. I don't remember if it was two or maybe three times week, but when it was all said and done, they said I had an IQ of 121. They talked about how strange that was because normally when a person has a head injury like I had they lose half of their IQ points. It became a point of contention that maybe I was too smart for my own good before the shooting.
>
> I don't necessarily believe that, but it sounds good anyway. I think it was just God taking care of me. He took care of me during the wreck, the head injury, and many other things. I never was really a churchgoer, Bible thumper, gospel singer, or whatever you want to call it. In fact, when I was much younger, I had been quoted many times as saying that I didn't belong in church. Now I'm talking to you about believing... *How strange is that?*

I would occasionally come into the physical therapy room after my timeslot and exercise. You see, recently I had been able to open and close my left hand. Believe you me, this may sound insignificant to you, but in my world this was a big achievement. I had also been noticing some movement in my left shoulder, which I wanted to expand upon.

Well, I would go in and exercise my shoulder. It was mostly elevation to the side at that time, but it was movement and, to me, it was a huge development. D would sometimes be in the room to help me get weights on. When I say "*weigh*ts", you may think of 1 pound or maybe 5 pounds. I started off with <u>2 ounces</u> and I guarantee you it was more than enough for my shoulder at the time.

    I wouldn't often come in after hours, but D would always see me when I did. The act itself of doing more therapy than wasn't required was a giant-size breakthrough. You see, at Salt Lake City ME (the physical therapist) and I would have long discussions about my recovery because I didn't want to get better. I had a fear of letting the same thing happen again, if you'll recall.

    "Ears full of tears", he would call it. Laying on my back, my tears would always fall into my ears. Oh, how I would fight him to do therapy. My Dad never realized that our home therapy sessions were so emotionally turbulent for that very reason. He would have to make me mad doing it, which was never any good for either of us. By the time our therapy sessions were over, we would both be in tears.

    The rehab hospital in Houston was different, however. It really did more for me mentally than physically. I had school there too. We would occasionally go on outings recreationally in a van that they called the *Blue Goose*. My counselor was not liked by Mom and Dad, because they thought she was turning me against them. I guess that you could say that was true to some degree.

    I have no idea what their relationship with the woman was. The only thing I know is that she was trying to get me ready to face the present and future. Doing this one thing from where I was at when I started with her was a giant task. Although I was fully aware, cognitive, or however you want to phrase *"self aware"*, I was also dealing with issues of unworthiness, inability, and being retracted.

I hid my private thoughts as I had done before. I needed the emotional and mental build up the rehabilitation center and the counselor provided at the time. Such things as being put into my first power chair, which I controlled with my chin and head movements, was a big event in my life. I got to where I would wander the halls, even though Mom and Dad were around a lot of the time.

> Imagine a blind person suddenly being given sight or a deaf person suddenly hearing... to me, being able to move myself around was phenomenal. It was an awakening for me into the land of the living.

All too often people take their daily lives and abilities for granted. When you can see what it's like from the other side, it gives you a great *(perhaps greater than normal)* appreciation of God's gifts to us.

Ever since the head injury, I have had trouble even urinating. The first time it occurred was at the University of Utah Hospital. I was barely able to whisper, was wearing an external catheter that was affixed on the outside of the penis and I only knew that I felt the urge to pee. The problem was, I couldn't. Time went by that felt like hours with me whispering, *"Piss,"* to the best of my ability.

I didn't know what was going on and I could barely utter that one word. They put me in the chair and pushed me around in the hospital. I started crying, saying, *"Piss,"* the best that I could. Oh yes, they questioned me, but I could barely utter that one word and didn't know anything else to say. The pain got unbearable and I was a red-faced, teary-eyed, immature, teenager then.

Finally, they got the idea to empty my bladder artificially with a tube *(catheterization)*. I didn't know about the process, but I understood the gist. Observing the nurses prepare everything eased my mind. When that nurse actually inserted the tube, I had that pleasant feeling of, ahhh... *It was great!*

In the Houston rehab, unfortunately for me, the power chair I was driving had two speeds high and low and as luck would have it, the indicators were reversed. I had to learn to drive the power chair on high speed. It was jumpy and touch-and-go there for a while. It was only after breaking a toe by slamming into a metal doorframe that the occupational therapist began to wonder if I was up to the task of driving the chair.

Mom and I were playing UNO in the recreational room with a lady called *"Pinky" (probably a nickname)*, the activities coordinator, when she noticed that my speed indicator twirled. That's when we discovered that I had actually been driving a Lamborghini instead of the VW bug that I was supposed to be learning on.

From there on, I was driving the chair a lot better.

3 Lifetimes In 1

When they finally gave me a license, so to speak, for driving the thing, I would tour the rehab facility at my leisure.

I saw things that most people wouldn't believe could happen in this day and age. At the onset, I considered my shared bedroom accommodations to be lackluster and plain. In this high dollar facility, I saw 20 people that were bed confined all in one room. They had no windows and no real space for themselves. It was amazing to me that some people called this humane. It reminded me of Third World countries. It was clean but that was the best feature.

From those few moments when I had the chance to view things from another perspective came an entirely different opinion of my life. I saw that a lot of us are so very fortunate. Those things and others that I saw enlightened me to the world reality between the have's and the have not's. I began to see the world much differently than I ever had before and I thank God for opening my eyes.

> Folks, what I saw would be considered a good life to a lot of people in other countries. In India or Egypt, for example, the simple, clean water that we have here in the United States would be considered virtually unobtainable to most of the population. *Think about it... Empathize with it...*

In the rehab hospital, there was one nurse's aide that I will never forget. Mother and Daddy had left for the evening and I had my shower by V. Now, she and I had several disagreements, mostly based in the fact that she thought I needed more care than most. That night was going to be her revenge.

She was particularly in a bad mood that night. Not much was said between us during my shower and then we returned to the room and put my external catheter back on. That deserves a little explanation; a latex external catheter is affixed to the penile shaft with what they call skin bond, which is kind of a glue, and a foam strap fastened around that.

Well, I thought all was well and went to sleep. When my Mom came in the next morning, she saw that the strap was wrapped extremely tight and immediately pulled it off.

The end of my tallywhacker was a nice shade of deep purple. To make a long story short, we finally got the blood flowing again. Mom and Dad both said their pieces to the staff.

Not long after that, it got to the point at the Houston rehabilitation center that every weekend, I would spend with Mom and Dad in their apartment. *That was truly a pleasure!* We would watch movies, go to theatres, malls, shopping centers, and do all kinds of different things.

Dad bought us a VCR which he and I loved playing with. We would record and watch things from Star Trek to Bonanza and assorted movies. Endless hours were spent with all three of us having fun.

From the rehab hospital to home in the apartment was a different mental state for me altogether, going there was a welcome relief from the dank dreariness of that rehab hospital.

I appreciated Mom and Dad more as time went on and

the time in that apartment made me respect all the things that they had done before that. I don't think I could have ever appreciated the concept of home and family as much without the Houston rehabilitation center. It allowed me to grow mentally and emotionally in giant steps.

When we came back from a weekend of fun at the apartment, the head nurse was the one I saw first. I asked her who was giving me a shower that night. When she said V, I felt like I had ice-water in my veins. I felt my innards seize up and my face run cold. Dad must have seen this because as I headed to my room, he had a little powwow with the head nurse. I don't know what went on in their conversation, but V was never assigned to me again.

I pulled a little stunt one day in physical therapy. D had me propped on my stomach and doing head lifts to try and strengthen my back. Well, I was doing repetitions of 10 and I sometimes skipped a number. Stupid stunt, I know, but, hey, I was a 17-year-old trying to have some fun. Anyway, I teased her saying I was skipping and she didn't notice. *(dumb again)*

She made a snippy remark about I was only hurting myself. She was right, of course. I may be thick-skulled, but I recognize truth when I hear it. It made feel bad because instead of looking at therapy from a healthy perspective *(and, by this time, I had grown beyond my defeatist Utah attitude)*, I was acting childish. Regardless, we both went on without incident and without play.

A few weeks later I was being discharged. I never realized why until ten or so years later when Mom and I were talking. In the course of our conversation, she tells me that it was D who was instrumental in my being pushed out of that rehab. Her opinion was that I wasn't really trying.

Immediately I thought of that pranky incident between us.

I went home from the Houston rehab sullen and maybe a bit wiser.

10

Going On

We went back to Merryville for a month or two and lived with my granny again while Dad and Mom decided our next move. During that time and the time before, my Granny and I became very close.

She was a careful observer of people as was my Dad, but whereas he judged by the way that they dressed, face, and carried themselves, Granny observed mostly on their actions and her feelings. She would sit back and simply remain quiet. By remaining distant in her manner, she would learn more about people than they ever knew themselves.

When it comes to my relating to others, I became a fairly quiet person because the head injury left me with a speech impediment. People around me would get used to me not talking and would often falsely dismiss my cognitive abilities just like my Granny. I tell you, the things you learn that way are sometimes surprising and even scary.

NOTE:
(Through college, my writing, and my public service, I've pulled out of some of my quietness.)

People have no idea what they reveal about themselves in their daily living. Dad and I, long ago, would sit in the van while Mom went in stores and he would teach me his methods. We would talk about people going in and coming out of different places and do judgment work on their characteristics.

It was generally a lot of fun and since we couldn't bond fishing or hunting together like we used to, it was a good time for us to meet together and share ourselves with one another.

We moved to Nowhere, Louisiana when Dad was working on a paper mill in Donaldson. It was not very far from the house. I don't guess it was a bad job for him, at least he never complained. That's it about Dad. He was a gentle spirit and very nurturing.

Soon after we got settled, I started counseling with Ms. F. I loved her to death. Over the 2 1/2 years that I met with her in the counseling about my past and how I ever got to the point of attempted suicide, I learned a lot of things about the point that I was at and some things about how I got there. Some things I kept secret even from her and probably never will tell another person as long as I live. Mainly because those memories are too dark, but there are other reasons why I must keep them hidden. I know of them and Ms. F taught me the skills that I needed to keep my sanity when dealing with these things.

I cannot tell you that it's been easy by any definition, and in fact, it has been damn hard, but as the years go by it gets somewhat easier. You get used to dealing with people that have questions about the issues, but some things never change. I not only know this for myself, but others have told me things about their experiences with the issues involved and we all agree that some of those remnant things never go away.

Most of the time I would go in by myself to talk to this counselor, but sometimes I could see Mom, Dad, or both were having trouble with some issues that I was not privy to and, to tell the truth, I didn't really want to know. On those occasions, I would let them go in with the counselor.

It helped. It really helped. They would come out feeling refreshed just as I would. Ms. F was a gentle spirit, just like Dad, and I found talking to her easy. I found talking to her about my issues *(and there were a lot)* just made things better.

Privacy became a big issue for me at one point. It was because I had so little of it. Mom and Dad tried the best they could to afford me all the privacy that they could, but when you're essentially incapacitated and dependent on others for everything that means that if you hide anything, it has to be hidden for you. If you want a snack, somebody has to get it for you. If you want to be clean, someone had to clean you, this means your face, hands, butt, and privates.

It's one of the biggest issues that I see over and over again in the quadriplegics that I've met over the years. You always have to depend on somebody to make sure that you are clean, fed, and taken care of in every respect. A quadriplegic has to take care of many more things that they actually have no control of than do able-bodied people. One-inch could mean the difference between reaching something you'll need and being deprived until someone else comes. It really is a lot to keep track of and much more than most people do to manage in their daily life.

Anyway, while I was seeing the psychologist, I also got into homebound school as a sophomore. They had first assigned me a girl named TE. She was sweet, and a good homebound teacher, but she only came once or twice a week and for a guy that wanted to learn that was just not enough.

You see most schools treat their homebound students

3 Lifetimes In 1

as a stopgap. By most definitions, it is a temporary measure until the student can get back into school. For me though, the school, to a large degree, was not accessible or right for my situation. You see, I wanted to learn, but was not either physically or emotionally capable of handling the rigors of either dealing with peers or handling the task-related stress. Some would say that wasn't quite right, but looking back, I think that's a correct assessment.

TE did help me get past my sophomore year, which I only had about three months left of and then because of personal problems, she left the school system but did return once to bring me a present of a Spanish verb conjugation book. It was her hope that I would continue with my Spanish since I enjoyed it so much. Alas, I didn't continue with Spanish, although I still hope to get back into it one day

---

When it came time for the school year to begin again, they set me up with another teacher who was fabulous, MH. She came out three times a week *(staying longer)* at first, I think. She and I got to know each other extremely well. We talked about her family, my family, my past, her past, the future, and every subject that you can think of.

She was a jolly person with two kids with all sorts of similar issues that I had. She came from a background of special education in the school system and knew exactly the kinds of issues that I was dealing with and would be dealing with in the future. She probably knew better than I did what kind of a world awaited me on the outside of the house.

Mark Wayne Allen

During the break from my junior to senior year, M came out to our house and worked with me, *possibly without pay*, because she knew it was necessary in order for me to graduate with my class. I think I got maybe two weeks of summer vacation that year. It was okay with me because I was doing the work at my own time and speed. *I've always liked to learn.* Dad always said, *"knowledge is power" (with all due respect to Schoolhouse Rock).*

My senior year we moved to a nearby home that was in a different school district. That particular district didn't want to allow MH to be my homebound teacher, but, being the person that she was, she finally told them that she would teach me for no pay if they would just allow her to continue with me so that I could graduate with my class in Nowhere.

This is to say nothing of the one physical class that Nowhere made me attend on the premise that I had to in order to graduate. *Boy, that was a disaster!* Not only was the ramp way too steep, but there was a cement pole blocking part of it. This is to say nothing of the classroom itself.

The class was a free-for-all! I couldn't even hear the teacher. Paper airplanes going into the air, spitballs, talking, etc... I think it was noisier than the engine of a 747.

The guidance counselor that had mandated the class was also the one who was holding up my assignments and didn't tell us when it was time to apply for scholarships. MH had to go to the teachers and beg for my assignments almost by saying, *"Hey, this kid wants to learn!"*

---

3 Lifetimes In 1

Finishing high school was important, yes, but during that time I was afraid of even getting beyond the front door of the house. I imagine that every new person that's wheelchair-confined is sensitive about the public at large. *In my case, it was much more of a factor.* I had committed what many consider the one unthinkable act that a human could never do. I was truly afraid of being judged in general and would rather crawl into my bedroom and turn off the light. Becoming a recluse sounded really good, but life was staring me in the face each day.

I tried lying to myself about many things, but the reality of my chair and my physique was staring me in the face every day. Fortunately, I had a Mom and a Dad that would take me to Walmart and buy me gifts as a reward for getting out. The only hitch was that I had to actually go in and pick out my reward. Sometimes it would be a trip to Pizza Hut or a movie that I was interested in. They would do just about anything to get me out.

I could not escape from reality too long. It was always staring me in the face and Mom would be joking and uplifting about all things. She was, and still is, is a lot of fun to be around except when she's in a bad mood. A rare thing... She would make my outings into a series of games. We would play, 'I Spy', count cars, count different license plates, or anything to keep my mind busy.

We would go to fishing at ponds that I could get right up to. Dad was always on the lookout for places that I could get up to the water and fish. Troy's pond was quite a distance from our house, but there, I could get very near the water.

I will always remember one of the most important and selfless acts that my Dad ever did. I was still in the Houston rehab and somehow, I'm not sure if it was near Christmas or what, but we started shopping for a new stereo for me. We had looked at a lot of them in the malls and shopping centers. We finally narrowed it down to two that I was torn between.

One, I think, was in JC Penn's and it was in a nice cabinet and virtually had everything that I wanted for around $400. The other was in this hole in the wall store filled with a lot of futuristic electronics. The name brand was AIWA and it operated almost strictly by squared, soft pushbuttons. The problem was that the system was $1,000, but it even had a turntable and cassette player that and could record from the push of one button. It was like nothing like anything I had ever seen or would ever see again. They were separate units that worked together, which I wanted. The amplifier had an automatic five-band equalizer.

Dad was determined to get it for me as like a motivational tool to try and get my arm moving more. My expert in stereos, G, came to visit during this process. I wanted him to look at things and give me his opinion. Unbeknownst to me at the time, Dad had privately talked to G and told him that no matter what I said, the AIWA was the right one to get.

Needless to say, it was the one Dad bought and, in hindsight, it was probably the much better choice to motivate me. I started off parking directly beside it and operating it with my little finger of the left hand. At first, it was hard, but

3 Lifetimes In 1

I wanted it and so I worked at it with great diligence. By the time I had completed my sophomore year with TE via homebound, I had gotten pretty decent at the operation of the system.

> Another way that Dad motivated me is in the process of laying me down in bed at night. He talked about Mom's nose a couple of nights while she was out of the room and then finally told me that he would give me $100 for punching her there. <u>That amount of money was a big deal in 1983!</u>
>
> *Well, it took me about eight months I suppose.* Raising my arm got easier and quicker every week. Slowly over that span of time, things improved to such a point that I was almost getting her nose each night and then came the night when I came a hair away from tagging her good. By *"good"*, I mean if it had landed, it would've brought blood. After I was settled for the night, Dad leaned over to me and told me not try anymore. I had earned that $100.
>
> I never saw that in cash, but he gave me so much more in love and gifts. I'm sure the AIWA stereo had my Mom's blessings as well. She became my friend, playmate, therapist, confidant, and whatever else. *They both were there for me more ways than I can say.*

It was about this time that the padding on my chin control for the chair started breaking down. We tried covering it with most everything that you can think of, to no avail. The material would just make my chin and face rather sticky and slimy. It was only when small pieces of it started coming off on my face did Mother blow her stack.

It was what you call, *"tough love"*, because I had talked about ordering another chin piece, but there is a caveat to the story. My chair was ordered with the chin control **and** a hand control.

Well, like I say, Mom blew her stack and told me she had had it with that chin control. It was the right thing to do and probably the right way to do it so that I would pay attention, but at the time, it was nerve-racking. I mean, she didn't fuss at me or anything, she was just disgusted at how that thing was doing my face and was fairly certain that I had enough arm movement to operate the hand control.

She had me go out into the garage where she dragged out that hand control, as well as some tools, and took the chin control off and put the other on. Afterward, *she told me to drive*. With my heart pounding about exploring new territory, I did as instructed.

After a few minutes of this, she set out obstacles of bricks for me to dodge in and out of. As the time went on, I got more comfortable and she did too. By the time that we went in the house, she was relaxed and, I was a more proficient driver. I was not skilled with the joystick yet, but good enough.

> In hindsight, her decision to change from the chin control to the joystick must have been gut-wrenching for her. *What if she had assessed my abilities wrong?* Sometimes our guts know better than our brains, but we need to temper those decisions with good judgment.

Ever since the first catheterization while I was in the University of Utah rehabilitation center, voiding has been a habitual problem. The first time that I would void in the mornings would always be the most problematic. I would sometimes spend hours in bed just trying to pee. Mom and Dad, if they were in the house, would try to remain still and quiet during my turbulent periods of trying to do a task that would come so easy to most everyone else.

Back then, even if I had voided that morning, it was no guarantee that I could do so for the rest of the day. Sometimes we would be in the middle of a mall and I would tell them that I needed to be catheterized. It would be painful and not to mention that I'd have to break off from doing something that was fun in order to relieve the pains of not being able to void.

Sometimes it wouldn't be something that was fun for me, but recreational for Mom and Dad. For instance, there were a few times when we were all able to break off and go somewhere for an overnight stay. They would lay me down in bed and position me as best they could and, during the night, I would start having trouble voiding.

By the time that everyone woke up, I would be in trouble. Over time, I found that, no matter how painful it was, that if I got up immediately, my odds of not having to catheterize would decrease to about 50-50. For me, that was darn good odds back then. It took me a long time and a lot of hours of concentration to even come to that conclusion.

> My waiting until they woke up was more a matter of courtesy for them. You see, people have to help me do about 90% of things. As a quadriplegic, I am unable to drive myself or do most things that people do so a lot of times I will delay needs or desires if they are not immediate. I have to take into account that my life impacts others. The Bible teaches respect for others as well as patience and I try to adhere to those high standards.
>
> To a large degree, I empathize with the people around and try to be sensitive to their needs as well as my own.

High school graduation was coming up. My counselor, Ms. F, was retiring and wanted to release me from all mental care. In fear, I suppose, I told her that I wanted to continue for a while even though both of us thought I was ready to be released so she recommended another therapist. I saw him a total of three times, I think, but it just wasn't the same and all the things that we were talking about had been long settled so I graciously bowed out.

Then came probably the biggest decision that most people make in their lifetimes, *what do I do with my life?* On the front end, I guess I always wanted to be a writer of sorts. I was heavily into computer programming at the time, so the decision to do that at Louisiana Tech was a natural one. Only, it wasn't at Louisiana Tech. It was at Louisiana Tech's Biomedical Engineering Department. Vocational rehabilitation would pay the fee for the handicap dorm and Mom and Dad were responsible for the rest.

> **God bless them, they didn't shy away one bit.**

So, I went up there and stayed for about 21 months *(originally 18 months, but I stayed an extra three to study something else)*. During my stay there, I saw people who were spinal cord injuries, cerebral palsy, muscular dystrophy, and just about everything else that you want to name.

We were supposed to study five programming languages, but we pretty much only studied two, and got minimal exposure to another three.

During the first quarter, the living conditions there were bad. You could smell urine from the bathrooms and just all manners of unsavory and unhealthy living conditions. *Mom and Dad to the rescue again!* I forget what they call it but there's a group of people that act as intermediaries in situations like that. They came in and arbitrated on our behalf.

Things got quickly better with no backlash from the upper management. They seemed to understand that things in the dorm were not as they should be and perhaps were already in the process of changing things for the better.

Mark Wayne Allen

Kudos go to them! Of course, it was diplomatic to do so.

It was early in my dorm life, I think my second or third quarter, that people were talking to me about the Bible. Now, I always believed in the Bible, its stories, and themes, but as to actually going to church or getting involved, I had not done any of that. I only had the brief time before the shooting that I actually read much of the Bible. It was not for a lack of trying, you understand. I had the children's Bibles and the Bible that was given to me after I had the burn, but I had always felt like the serene atmosphere of a church was not right for me. I didn't belong there.

Dad had bad experiences with the church atmosphere when he was growing up. He always made sure that he talked to me about the Lord on fishing trips, hunting, or any occasion where he could bring up the subject. He also knew more about the Bible than most people I've ever known. *An uncommon man, to be sure.*

Anyway, with a great many people in the dorm all inviting me to go to church with them combined with sharing a dorm room with a devout, church going person avoiding the issues were hard. Add to that his best friend was the son of a Baptist preacher. He was studying theology in order to become a preacher himself. The two friends would talk about the Bible a lot and since I was in the room too, it became a hard thing to ignore.

They also had this guy living in the dorm named J. He was a paraplegic and didn't really need the aide's help *(he soon moved out but made many return trips to visit)* who knew the Bible backwards and forwards. Although he didn't mean to, J brought a great deal of pressure on me to state what I believed. He talked to me about this issue, that issue, and what about this issue over here…

It was really getting hard on me when the unthinkable happened. I had been seeing a doctor named QQ and he gave me Ampicillin for a bladder infection that I had. I stopped by the office on the way out just on a hunch and asked about the medicine because it sounded too much like Penicillin, *which I am allergic to*. They said it was totally different so I went on and started taking the pills.

I took two pills in all before I spoke to Mom and Dad that night. Mom told me not to take anymore until I heard from her. <u>Ampicillin, if you don't know, is a synthetic version of Penicillin</u>.

Well, I suffered for two days until I called home and asked to be picked up. My Dad saw me the next morning he told me later that he freaked out. I was running fever and had a rash, had been to the emergency room, and was generally feeling pretty lousy.

Dad got my things together and we went home. My regular doctor said that the rash was on the inside as well as the outside. Dad wanted to go beat that Dr. to a bloody pulp, but didn't, but within about four or five days, I was on my way back up to the college.

It was just me and Dad going up there and I talked to him about the religious pressure that I was being put under. *I think he gave me some good advice*. He told me to simply decide what I believed and then stick to it. We talked for a long time about the issues, but that's what it boiled down to.

So when I got up there, I approached everyone with a firmer stance than what I had been. Oh, I did visit several different churches up there, that includes a Lutheran Church, which my friend G was in, but none of them really felt right for me. *It was enough to keep the peace with everyone though.*

My brother was working at a radio station during some of my stay at Tech and he sent me two tapes with narration and theme songs from the shows and songs that we grew up with. *They were hilarious!* They were a welcome reprive from the drudgery of school. An Aunt sent me a care package while I was up there too.

I never will forget those things. They meant an awful lot to me.

> **Here I was, just a quadriplegic and people were sending me stuff to keep me going. It was much appreciated!**

After completing the courses, my brother found out that there was not going to be any *"per se"* graduation ceremony. I was told that they would just hand me the certificate of completion and then they would send me on my merry way.

To Michael, that just wouldn't do. His marketing business was celebrating an opening of some sort just a few days later and he made part of that celebration be my graduation ceremony. The department heads from the biomedical engineering department came down and handed me the diploma in a grand Gala of events that went on that weekend.

I was very honored that he would do that for me.

> From college, I moved back to yet another new place. It was not so bad this time as I was coming home a college man. I had become *"road tested"* and had done well other than the aforementioned illness and having testophobia *(or test'itis)*.

I was at the end of my course in Computer Literacy and took the test. I busted it, *flunked.* The computer classes were on an A or F grading scale and I blew it. That night I called home depressed and feeling like a failure in every way. They were going to retest in a few days, but I wasn't confident of passing.

The next day, my wonderful Mother drove up to Ruston, La., a three-hour drive, to talk to me. Her mere presence was calming to me. As my Mom, she knew exactly how exasperated I was. We met in the observation room at the dorm where nobody went and she began thumbing through my book and she started asking me different questions. At first, I fumbled for words for just about everything she asked. Then she laid her hand down on me and told me to calm down by taking several deep breaths.

She then began asking me different questions again. *I was slow and cautious this time.* The more she asked me, the more I felt comfortable, and I began answering correctly for every question. She looked at me with soft eyes and told me that these were things that I had been quoting to her throughout my high school years. I agreed and saw light at the end of the tunnel for the first time in many days.

I asked her to stay and visit awhile, but she politely told me that she had to get back. It dawned on me then that she had driven three hours one way and now was going to drive three hours back home merely to calm me.

<u>How great is that???</u> I was in awe.

"Road Tested." I was coming home having proven to myself and everybody that I could pass the classes. I could survive the consequences of life and all the little nuances that comes as a person. Well this is not quite true as I came to find out in later years, but, all in all, Lafayette was a good place to return to.

Having gotten educated in computer technology, Dad said, *"Okay, son, you have this education so now you're going to need a computer to work with."* After a long search, with visitation with old friends in between, we finally selected a computer to buy. As we found out after a few days, we had to change out the Motherboard ourselves via direction over the phone. *Dad was very nervous*, but did as told by the technicians and we got the problem corrected. <u>I really commend him!</u>

Soon, I started looking for a job. I would've had one, had I known C+ *(That's a programming language).*

3 Lifetimes In 1

> Unfortunately, it was not to be. Not being able to find a job was disheartening. Especially after going through all that time and expense. For this reason, I went on a self-training program. I didn't know it at the time but it would last 2 1/2 years.

We did a lot of fishing with friends though at the Delcom intercoastal waterway. You see, I would hook the fish and Daddy would reel them in. I, we, caught a 15-pound catfish that way. Mom caught a 26-pounder!

It wasn't long after that before we moved to Baton Rouge.

> At this point, I would like to backup and explain something. In addition to all the doctors that I would see every now and then, I was in therapy constantly. In Wyoming and Merryville it would be just Dad and I and we fought like cats and dogs. He had no idea what was going on in my head and I'm not sure even to this day that I realize everything. That's a heck of a statement. I'm the one that lived it. I should know it best. I suppose I understand it best of anybody, but as to really saying I know everything that happened and why it happened, I still haven't a clue.
>
> Anyway, at Louisiana Tech, I would have therapy at the hospital with a man named JC. **He was actually the best therapist that I've ever had**. He knew how to mentally motivate me and he knew all the technologies best suited for me better than anybody else ever has. There are not many

> things that I regret about leaving Louisiana Tech in Ruston, but I really didn't want to leave him.

When we moved to Baton Rouge, first it was BRM. The therapist there kicked me out the door in three short months, but she and I had, how shall I say it, irreconcilable differences. She wanted simple strengthening, I wanted the whole package.

After that debacle, I went to RR and there I stayed for a long time. They wanted the same things that I did, but I think that how they went about it the whole thing was skewed and wrong for me. Finally, the therapist came to me and said that she didn't feel like I was progressing. I just said okay and then went on to another place that was much bigger and that had recently opened.

I finally thought that I had found the place that was going to do the right things to get me in shape, but after three months they released me.

> **By the time they said that, I had been released by many facilities and had given up trying to find the *"right"* rehab that would do the things that I knew needed to be done. It was frustrating and I don't know if my methods would have worked and I never will.**

Anyway, I just told them that I had been at this a long time and knew that there was no malice intended.

I had been searching for a therapist like JC, but what I

really found was places that were mainly interested in making money. JC had me on a tilt table for a while to strengthen me and then got me on a mat, just like he did at first, and had me try to crawl around. He knew from the first time that he had me on the mat that what I really needed was strengthening at first, then we'd move on to mobility.

I can tell you for sure that the first time I was screaming and wailing like a baby. The pain and discomfort were pretty extreme. The second time, which was about four months later, sure I was grunting, but I was doing my best at crawling. I had a goal in my mind and the strength to handle the positioning.

The last three months that I was with JC, he had me standing in a walker with a platform on the right side to support my weak arm. He had even prompted me to take a step. The eventual plan we had discussed was to put braces on my legs, but first I had to develop my back muscles to the fullest extent.

> I feel that I could've eventually regained much of my abilities if I had been able to stay with him, but, alas, it was not to be.

After living in Baton Rouge for about a year and a half, vocational rehabilitation meets with me and says, *"Hey, we'll help you go back to college at LSU."* I didn't really want to go back to college all over again, it was grueling work the first time. Mom was all for it. Dad said it was education that we would have help paying for. Me, I didn't want to go through all that work again and come out on the other side in the same situation. Little did I know…

Long story made short, back to college I went. This time in business... In particular, my major was business management. About a year and a half in, I toppled out of our van lift, which I swear to this day had a problem of some sort. Normally, I would go and hit the flaps at the end, which would stop me. Well, it didn't stop me this time and I flew off, feet first, about four-feet down into the concrete parking lot.

The X-rays showed two broken legs and the orthopedist that was on call didn't *"feel"* that two broken legs were "important enough" for him to come down from his hill top and take care of the little people. **JERK!** According to the x-rays, the bones were perfectly in line that night. They packed my legs in ice and I spent the night trying to make my body, which ever since the head injury had (and still has) vigorous muscle spasms, be still. By the time that the jerk walked in the next morning, soreness had set in. When they took some fresh x-rays, the bones in my right leg had separated.

Well, the decision was, and it was my decision as well, since I was not going to be walking on my legs, to just set them, as they were. Deep in my gut there was a sick feeling like time had slipped away. Up until that point, I had always believed that with the right therapist and the right program that I could get up walking again.

3 Lifetimes In 1

Time had caught up with me. That orthopedist plainly told all of us that the way the bone would heal that it would never stand up to pounding of walking. If only that jerk had come the night before...

As an orthopedist, he actually turned out to be pretty nice.

> I dropped out of college for that semester which was pretty good anyway since I was taking an astronomy class with the worst teacher in the world. I swear, the guy would stand up and write on the blackboard the entire class without explaining anything. Some teacher, huh? I was going to have to have a long chat with him because it was too late to change classes. Some teachers are better than others. That's for sure.

To make a long story short, I spent six of the toughest years of my life at LSU adapting to whatever situation that they threw at me. I was in a four-year program that actually was five years, six if you went full-time only and did not take any extra hours, and graduated in 1996.

My last two semesters, I went on absolutely every interview that I could trying to get a job. The closest I came was JC Penny's and some business that was three hours away from where we lived. I finally decided that as a quadriplegic, that my chances of working on a *"normal"* job were horrible. Everybody told me that I gave a good interview, but nobody wanted me.

Mark Wayne Allen

> Skilled in computers, bachelors degree in business management, road tested, independent, and all that wasn't enough. *Or was it just me?* I have often wondered. Even my counselor at vocational rehabilitation was stumped and scratching her head in search of answers.

Within about eight months the opportunity for moving back to Merryville came up. Granny, who had been, other than Mom and Dad of course, my emotional rock was suffering from health problems.

NOTE: *I learned from Mom that when Granny heard that I was in need, she would send nurturing Angels for my spirit and warrior Angels to fight for me. Namely these were my critical junctures such as John Peter Smith, Salt Lake City, Houston, Baton Rouge, Ruston, and I'm sure there were many more critical times.*

The value of these things was something that I would realize soon in my life.

We did end up moving back to my hometown of Merryville and into Granny's house. Granny had had breast cancer years earlier and there had recently been another tumor that had been removed, I think the smallest on record. *It was malignant.* As a result, she was put on all kinds of cancer drugs, which I think contributed to her mental problems, but, Granny, still being in her right mind, donated her house to Mom and Dad.

> I turned 33 shortly after they opened their Mom and Dad opened their gift shop in Merryville. It was interesting, but I was going through a major crisis as you will see.

Mark Wayne Allen

11

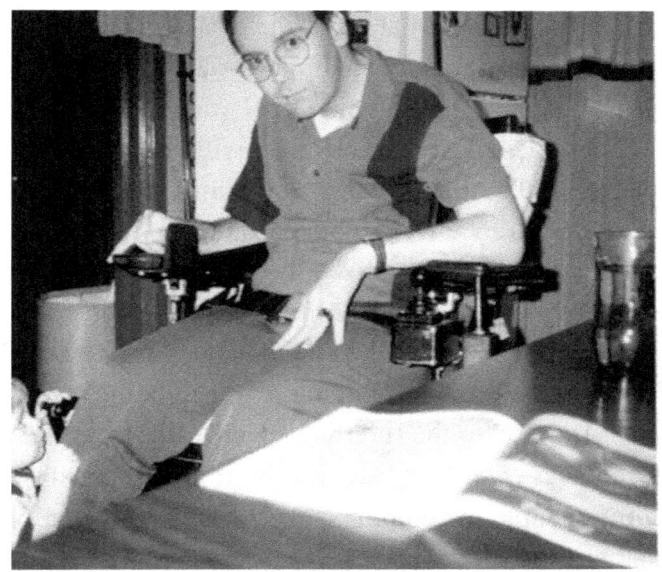

Life Revelation

There came a period of self-reflection that needed to happen. I suppose that most people whose lives are not settled as far as home, spouse, and most of the things that we pursue as, *"our keys to happiness,"* go through this. The ages may differ, but what we all want is to have long-term happiness and to live a joyful life. Right?

For me, the age where my dreams didn't fit my lifestyle was 33. You see, while others go out and meet people at the local convenience store, grocer, retailer, gas station, or other, but these were not a *"real"* option for me. As a quadriplegic, I didn't drive and didn't even go out much. The only female companion that I ever had was my aide and a woman that I had met at LSU that I had lost contact with.

<u>My only reasonable option was the Internet</u>. Mom and Dad would've taken me wherever I wanted to go, but I was not about to suggest that they stay with me while I flirted or leave me at the mercy of this sometimes cruel world. It also makes a difference when you live in a very small town with not many places to socialize anyway. Plus, talking with people implies a reason to communicate: work, friends, common subjects, etc. I had none or very little experience with common life except being a human being.

I turned to the Internet, specifically personal ads. The Internet was *(and is)* a low risk, high involvement way of meeting people, women in specific. Low risk meant that I didn't have to meet everybody in person and take chances on deceptive people. The high involvement part of it needs a bit of explaining to people who are not tech savvy.

On the Internet via the written really lets you get to know someone from the inside and out. They talk to you about what they are feeling and what they are actually like inside. Nowhere else except maybe letter correspondence can you do that. And a lot of people have said to me, but a person can lie to the four-winds when it is not face to face. Maybe so for an expert liar, but in 99% of cases of people who are being deceptive about themselves, you can tell that they are lying. If you've never gotten to know people this way, it's very hard to describe.

Most people won't believe me, but it's true. If you're very observant and feel your way, you'll see what I'm saying. Because of that, out of the 200 or more people that I chatted with, I only decided to meet four of those in person.

> **These days, it's a lot easier. People can use Skype and all kinds of other things.**

Like I say, I was in a life crisis. I had reserved going out and seeking women for when I thought that I wouldn't move anymore. Traveling a lot as I did growing up, I guess made me a little bit gun shy about developing relationships. That is not to say that I would give anything for the well-rounded, overall view of the world that I do have. **Nay.** I think that the robust, detailed view of the world that I have been afforded allows me to put myself anywhere mentally and adapt myself to the surroundings.

That, in itself, allows me to be a better writer and empathizer with people, things, and situations. It is not an easy life to be moving around all the time, but it is rewarding. I have seen a lot of beautiful things and experienced a lot of different situations such as camping out in the mountains, fishing in creeks as well as mountain streams, hunting in warm and cold climates, and many other things.

I had explored three people that I had met on the

Internet and none came even close to working out. Meanwhile, Mom and Dad had gotten involved in a local church and Mom was continually asking me to go. Her questions quickly became insistent talks.

Now, I had always had an aversion to church, any church, I don't know why. After the wreck, the whole family went to the visiting pastor's church from John Peter Smith Hospital, where I was for the burn. I don't know why we stopped going, but I remember feeling uncomfortable there. *I have no idea why.*

After the head injury, my aversion became an obsession. I had went to church with friends of mine at Louisiana Tech simply to keep the peer pressure at bay. Those services, were not really what I would consider church at all and I shall not delve into that. I was there only in body anyway, not in spirit. I had insulated myself completely from any context of the services. *Now, things were different.* There is a unique difference from outside pressure (friends, classmates, etc.) and family members whom you love and want to do right by. So, finally I said yes that I would go with them to church.

That would be the day of my unraveling. I had knots in my stomach that whole night before that fated Sunday morning. We woke up, got ready, and were out the door all too soon. Everybody at the church welcomed me and we quickly took our seats. I was feeling nauseous, but I made it through the first two songs fine.

The third song was Amazing Grace which I have always had a sensitivity to because the message is such a beautiful one that although we are as filthy rags, we all look perfect in His eyes. In a few moments, I turned my chair around and made a dash for one of the back rooms wishing that I could go out the door on my own strength. Instead, I turned into a room. I had no idea what it was for and, once I was around the corner, started crying my eyes out.

No one knew what happened on that day, not even me. A member of the church, VV, whom I had just met that day, came to me and tried to help me. I will forever be indebted to her for that. Little did she ever realize that in my life, as it was then, that was a big thing. The kindness of others is a powerful thing and very moving emotionally. Mother rushed back to settle me and then VV retook her seat.

It had never dawned on me until a few days ago what that episode was about and if I had not been writing this book, it probably still would've been a mystery. I was there physically and emotionally on that Sunday, for my Mom, and it was the proverbial immovable object meeting the unstoppable force. I had built up a barrier in my mind because in 1982 when I attempted suicide it conflicted with my own personal Christian beliefs. If I had not gone to church that day, those two things would probably still be mutually exclusive, but on that day, they collided.

The result was an emotional breakdown. It was cosmically significant for me. It allowed me to move past that blockade and recognize the miracles that had occurred in my life as what they really were. *Understand me though...* I had deep convictions about my Christianity even before that point, but when you're in the midst of trying to deal with major crises, you are just trying to deal with the facts that have occurred in the best way that you know how.

The best way to deal with something depends on the individual. For me, it was holding on for dear life to everything I knew. It was not easy and I still sometimes wonder how in the heck I made it through those things *(burn, head injury, gall bladder, kidney stones, and many others)* and still remain as sane as I am.

I soon went back into the main church room with my red face that shined like a lighthouse. You've met people that could cry for hours and afterward still pass for normal? Well, that's not me. I can cry for thirty-seconds and then everyone knows it the entire rest of the day.

I was like that as a kid too. I couldn't get away with nothing. My parents could see me coming from a mile off with the brightest red nose that you ever saw. I'm telling ya, Rudolph would have been jealous of my nose.

Well, I thought that was the end of it, *but no sirree*, that was not the end. It was more like that was just the tip of the iceberg. Getting back in church and feeling those things was bad enough, but I said before and I will say it again, living with attempted suicide is a horrible thing. I have evaded the issue in conversations by telling fibs and half-truths to avoid the subject.

3 Lifetimes In 1

About this time you might be asking yourself, *"Didn't the counseling take care of this discomfort?"* Yes, and no. The counseling taught me how to deal with it, live with it, and the techniques to never let myself be in that position again. In addition, it taught me problem resolution techniques and to not hold my feelings in. Dealing with others, to some degree, was included, but reality is a lifelong thing and no one, no matter who you are, can say that every situation that you face in your life is easy. Time brings us uncounted situations, each with their own intricacies.

> **Sometimes it would not be so hard, but most of the time it was frocked with thorns.**

I continued going to church with Mom and Dad and I felt a growing pull. What happened on that morning that I went to the altar this day is, and will forever be, debatable. My version of the story is that Dad, who was sitting right beside me, looked over at me and asked me if I would go to the altar with him. Well, *naturally I said yes*. He swore until the day he died that what he asked was that if he went down to the altar with me, would I go.

In either case, we both had the intention of helping the other. It amounted to me going down with him at my side. I quickly became the focal point of everyone mainly because I was crying and screaming like a baby within minutes. Until a few days ago I never realized why.

The first episode of crying, or release of emotion was

me actually breaking the invisible barrier abut actually going to church and being in the Lord's house. The second, and more vociferous, episode of me crying at the alter was about me coming to the Lord.

I have no idea what actually happened that day except to say what the result was. **Am I grateful that it happened the way it did? Yes!**

<u>Since then I have actively gotten involved in church.</u>

My Dad started Yellow Dog Incorporated shortly after that. It was and is a company that specializes in industrial heat treating equipment. When he started it, my Mom said it was the worst idea that he had ever had. **Ha** Now, she regrets her comment. While they started the company, I was still fooling around with online personal ads. I went out with three girls I think before my Mom talked to my doctor's nurse.
She was trying to get the results of my blood work. We had been finding it strange that I had been going every month to do labs for him. I can assure you that I have had more than enough needles stuck in me. I didn't want anymore and still don't. I have been stuck femoral, wrists, neck, and just about every other place you can think of. At one time, *"doctors"* had to draw my blood because I was such a hard stick.

Anyway, back to my story. So, my Mom calls and talk to the nurse. She lets it slip that my doctor is doing regular blood work because I had hepatitis. <u>Well, naturally, Mom freaks</u>. She demands to talk to the doctor and a little while later we get a call and the doc says that he wasn't worried about it. **Humph!**

Well, long story short, I dropped that doctor like very fast. I wanted a specialist and got into a hepatitis clinic. She was a nurse practitioner. Very sweet and very caring... She tells me that I had to undergo chemotherapy to try and rid myself of the disease. There were two hitches in the plan. One, the treatment was so expensive that nobody could afford it. Two, I would have to be in this treatment plan for a duration of 48 weeks.

Fortunately, she said that she was in a charity hospital and the main cost to us would be the monthly trips for follow-up visits.

Well, my chemotherapy treatment for hepatitis C is the only thing worth noting during that whole year. I really feel for anyone that has to go through that. I'm told that it's a lot easier now on the body. When I took the treatments, it was very very harsh and the nurse practitioner told me that rarely does anybody ever make it completely through the treatment.

I don't know why a blood transfusion from 1982 would take nearly 25 years to surface from its dormant state. I don't know and I probably don't want to know. ***Maybe it was strictly so that I could tell you this.***

Halfway into my treatments they did a viral count.

Now when I called the lab for the results it was a low number, but it wasn't clear. I would go to church where my brother was the pastor and for some reason he stopped right in the middle the service, brought me up, and then prayed for my healing. When I went to the nurse practitioner's office two days later, that viral count was undetectable.

> **Why the Lord would bless me again, I do not know.** He has blessed me in so many ways. I suppose that in a large way I'm giving you my testimony.

It doesn't have to be big things like this either. Ever since my head injury, if I had to go out and it was raining at the time, all of a sudden it would stop just long enough for me to get loaded into the van. After we were in the vehicle it would start raining again. Five minutes before I would have to get out, it would stop raining long enough for me to get out indoors, and then the bottom would drop out again.

> **Little things like that mean a lot and I never forget to thank the Lord for the favor.**

Well, like I say, the hepatitis really killed my year. By the end of the treatment, I would get up in the morning, sleep in my chair, eat lunch, sleep in my chair, and then lay down for the night. I was a rare one to have made it all away through and the nurse practitioner was so proud. *Thank God, I*

have been hepatitis free ever since.
   Wherever that nurse practitioner is, thank you and Bless you. The same blessing goes to the family doctor who saw me through that time in my life. The warmth and caring meant a great deal during that time.

> I got back into trying to expand my love life after the treatments. Six months later, I would meet my future wife.

Mark Wayne Allen

12

Final Words

You could almost say that when my future wife, Kelley, and I met, my life began such a dramatic change again that I would almost characterize it as Life Four. The simple reason is because as she and I fell in love *(and for me I think it was love at first sight)* I grew a self-confidence that I had never had since before the wreck.

It far surpassed my youth however.

We chatted, emailed, and talked on the phone for six months before we ever met face-to-face. After we met, we never looked back. During our *"togetherness" (I told her right from the start that I didn't "date" because of the connotation)* we traveled to movies, family events, and a whole lot more.

There's something that I need to say here. When you get to know a person as we did in written word rather than speech there is something magical that happens. You get to know the other person on the inside, which is who they really are. You see, although I was honest about my quadriplegia, speech problems, and the whole shebang right from the start, she had a chance to know me for who I really am on the inside *(hopes, dreams, attitudes, etc.).*

It's that remarkable thing that allowed us to fall in love right from the start. Well, I say right from the start... She went home and talked to a friend of hers and said, *"Well, there's this guy in a wheelchair that I've been talking to, but I don't see any future for us. I don't see me getting involved very much with him."*

That all changed when she received the dozen pink roses that I sent her. She had never had anyone send her flowers before.

I sent them for two reasons actually. One, to show her that I really cared about her. Two, that I wanted to further our relations. It's great to make someone feel nice if you can and I wanted her to feel wonderfully important to me.

We had even started making plans toward marriage during our chats and began to see each other more often. Six months later, I proposed.

She wanted to wait two years, *if you can believe that*, to get married. I was dismayed, at first, but as it turns out, we needed the extra time to buy a house and renovate it before moving in. Needless to say, we had a lot of troubles. Not with each other, but simply trying to refurbish the house.

I will say no more about our troubles, but do want to sum it up like this. Watch your back when dealing with contractors because the things that you think can't go wrong, have no idea can go wrong, and/or don't even know about, will go awry.

We were not even married three months before Hurricane Rita hit our home. We ended up in evacuating out of comfort and necessity because a power wheelchair needs electricity. While we were evacuated, I messed around and broke a finger. Well, we came home and my wife stepped out for a minute to go and visit someone. I go from the office of our house into the bedroom. Unbeknownst to me, the tip of my foot catches on the door.

If you know anything about wheelchairs then you know that the foot pieces unlatch and swing out to the side and from there they can be removed. Well, my foot piece was unlocked and my shoe caught on the edge of the door. I didn't realize this and so I continued forward until I felt a sharp pain right above my ankle. **Ouch!**

I knew it hurt like the dickens and that it took a long time for the pain to subside. I called over to Mom and Dad's house which was about three blocks away and both of them came to see about my issue. Dad, who had a lot of first aid training from his construction jobs throughout the years, felt of my leg and said he thought I was all right. We put ice on my leg for what we thought was a sprain.

After everybody had gone home, RC, my aide at the time, tried to lay me down in bed. We got to the bed, but I could not put that leg down on the bed without excruciating pain so we got back in the chair and headed to the emergency room.

<u>Yep! Broken leg.</u> They put my leg in one of those soft casts, boot, and because of my osteoporosis, it stayed on for nine months. I had always said that I was going to burn that boot when it finally came off, but it was so stinky by that time that it came off I just tossed it in the garbage.

> **I'm sure by this point that Mom and Daddy were thinking, "What in the world has this boy got into?"**

Kelley had gone all summer of our honeymoon summer looking for a job and I'm sure it was worrying her to death. Without her having a decent job, we would be financially insolvent.

Going through what I have been through sort of gives me a unique outlook on life. I always feel that the Lord is going to get us through. It was within a month of school time and she was almost frantic. I just took her by the hand and prayed with her. The Bible says that He takes care of the lilies of the field and they don't worry. They toil not and neither do they spin but the Lord care of them. I had faith that He would take care of us.

Two weeks before school was about to begin, news about a job nearby, in Texas, came up. She interviewed and was hired on the spot.

Two years later, her job in Texas as the band director was cut from the budget. *Here we go again.* We would go all summer without the security of a job to go to in the fall. Again, she was pretty high strung about the issue and deservedly so, but again I was reassuring.

Two weeks before school was to start, she got a job here in our hometown of Merryville. ***Is that God or what?*** He's an on-time God! All we can do is human beings is try our best. I say this to you and, yes, I worry too about some things. I'm a flawed human being just like everybody else.

When I started out to tell you about my loving wife is that she has a lot of strength. I know she loves me just by her actions such as, reaching for my hand, straightening my fingers, combing my hair, and generally caring for me the same as I do for her.

She had always had hormone trouble, or at least ever since I knew her, and as fortune would have it, about a year and three months into our marriage she was getting weaker and weaker. It was the doctor, Kelley, and I trying to work on her health, but about this time it was decided that she needed a hysterectomy.

We had known from the get-go that natural kids for us

may not have been an option. We were comfortable with the notion and, more than likely, knew it was going to be an eventuality. So about a year and half into our marriage, we all three, her gynecologist, Kelley, and I, got in the office together and spent over an hour trying to convince my bloodless *(white as a sheet)*, hardheaded wife that it was either do the surgery or die. This is how hardheaded my Kelley is! The only thing was, she didn't know that I have the hardest head in the world from the school of hard knocks.

So, she had surgery and me and her Mom spent days and nights with her until she was able to get up and out of the hospital. I think I surprised everyone by not leaving her to fin for herself, but that's just the way I am.

I'm very protective of family. That comes from my Dad who was very nurturing.

I just said I was hardheaded. S<u>ometimes too much so...</u> There was this old black cat that had been hanging around the house for weeks and I had been trying to drive it off ever since it arrived. Well, we came back after checking on my mother who had just had a mastectomy because of breast cancer. I guess it was about 11:30 PM. when we arrived at our home. I went up our ramp to the porch *(4 feet off above the ground)*. Now, there was this old black cat standing there and I swear it was laughing at me. Well, I turned my chair around and was going to scamper at it and, you know, to scare it off, only I didn't just charge at it. I charged off of the porch right into Kelley's corner garden..

It's laughable now, but at the time it was very serious. The next-door neighbor, who was outside at the time, came charging over and helped me get my chair up. After a trip to the emergency room, I came home with a badly jammed neck, a cracked knee, and a bruised ego.

> God took care of me, but I have never lived that down and I probably never will. Talk about merciless teasing...

I won't bore you with all the details of a marriage that is unique, but incredibly strong. Just let me say that Kelley and I have overcome tremendous difficulties and toppled the odds. *I love her so much!*

She also had to go into emergency surgery for kidney stones and then I had the same trouble, non-emergency. <u>Only with me</u>, things can never go easy. They couldn't get my stones the first time so I had to have two surgeries.

The death of my Dad was horrendous to me. He and my Mother were always the ones who stuck by me through incredibly thick and turbulent times and never gave up, no matter the odds or circumstances. He suffered a major stroke two years before he died. It was incredibly difficult for me to see him struggle as I have these many years.

That level of frustration against your own body is difficult to deal with. Daddy ended up barely able to move any part of his body. At least I have a left arm that I can use pretty well, but he didn't have even that much.

> Through everything that's ever happened to me, I haven't asked why. It is all in God's plans and He takes care of us. Like I have said before, I've just dealt with the circumstances that I've been faced with but I do wonder after all of Dad's support, why he had to suffer a similar fate as me.

Tragic episodes have reshaped my life time and time again. I don't know why and probably never will. I don't really want to know because, as my wife says, if it hadn't, her and I would probably not be together and I guess that says more than anything.

> You might say that I am more optimistic than most because of the times and predicaments that I've faced. My wife and I may not be rich, but we have it good enough. We can pay the bills and keep the wolves away. She's a teacher. I'm a city councilman in a town of about a 1,000 people. I also do computer/IT and, of course, write. We are in reasonable health and that counts for a lot as far as the ability to enjoy life.
> I'm still a quadriplegic, but do have fair use of my left hand and arm. I still suffer from posttraumatic stress disorder. That's something that never goes away, but I've been so very blessed by God through many more events than what is detailed in this book like a loving family, a roof over my head, reasonable health, good mental faculties, a great wife.

3 Lifetimes In 1

> *These are only a few of our blessings.*

Mother and I were in a slight collision when I was at Louisiana State University. It was not mom's fault and it took maybe 20-minutes for campus police to clear it up.

When we rode off and were approaching the main highway, we saw an overturned 18-wheeler. By the looks of things, if we had been at the intersection as if nothing had happened, we would've been involved the major accident instead of the minor one.

Sometimes bad things happen to us for **Good** reasons.

My roughest semester at LSU, I had to take four heavy weight, very rough, classes. Two of these were business statistics and accounting. I had gone to endless tutoring sessions in each and still had a D average. For a guy that was used to making A's & B's, this was heart breaking to me.

On the day after I got both tests back, I came home, went straight to my stereo, put some music on, and considered dropping out. That day, I was beaten and depressed because both grades were F's.

Well, after about two hours, in comes Michael with a song to play for me. Well, almost mindlessly I told him to go ahead. The song was *"Press On"* by <u>Billy Sprague</u>. He said that he was actually in bed and the Lord told him to bring that song to me. I accused Mother of telling him about my contemplation, but she said no.

You never know how God is going to help those that believe in Him. One thing is for sure, we must try our best. I urge you to put forth your best effort.

Life is what you make it, My Friends, so go forth into the world with a propensity to share the blessings of your life with everyone. My life has been eventful to be sure and however much that I have experienced bad things, I have seen that it could always have been worse. The knowledge has given me a peace of mind, a spirited nature, and other things that I cannot put into words. May you find your way as enlightened as mine, but hopefully without having to experience life the way I have.

I still look at my scarred skin, both burn and graft sites, get emotional, and even cry, but I know there is a purpose for everything that happens, both good and bad. I still think of those times after the wreck and pray for all those who were involved. I even wince from the emotions that those memories conjure up. I still think about the gunshot and suffer the lengthy emotionalism from the incident. All of this is just of part of major trauma. I have limited physical abilities and daily aches and pains as a result of life events. Mine is not to reason why but to trust in the Lord, to carry on, to keep moving forward.

May the blessings of God be on you and yours in the many years to come.

May you always trust in Him and move forward, whatever situation you face.

***

Mark Wayne Allen

Mark Wayne Allen published Star Siege in 2013. It was written while getting his bachelor's degree from Louisiana State University. Since that time, he has continued writing and become active in the community.
He actively publishes new items, but books have remained his focus. He and his wife, Kelley, have been happily married for 10 years in Merryville, La.

To this day, many of his writings still remain unpublished, but he hopes to make them available one day.

Website: http://markwayneallen.com
Blog: http://markwayneallen.com/blog/
Facebook: https://www.facebook.com/authormwa
Twitter: authormwa

> If you enjoyed this book, please rate it at Amazon.com.
> http://markwayneallen.com/review

Introspection
From The Melvin Time Chronicles

www.ingramcontent.com/pod-product-compliance
Lightning Source LLC
Chambersburg PA
CBHW050632300426
44112CB00012B/1761